ACKNOWLEDGEMENTS

This is the part of any book that no author likes writing, for within this section there is a great danger of missing someone out. If I have forgotten to name you here, then accept my apologies now but here goes.

Special mention must go to my partner Karen and the kids Victoria, Liam, Alex, Johnathon, Finn, Rory and Francesca who put up with my swinging moods as I have rewritten this book. Special thanks to Ian Parker for the critique on self and ownership that forced me to think through the chapter on the four self's'.

To Dr Terrence McLaughlin, thank you for the debates and discussions that have shaped much of my thinking. Marius Romme and Sandra Escher as always have been my inspiration in writing this book they more than any others have guided my thinking and I can never thank them enough. John Jenkins is also instrumental in the writing of this book, for he allowed me to develop my beliefs around recovery in practice.

Thanks also to Alison Reeves who wrote the booklet Recovery a Holistic Approach her booklet made me stop and think about the importance of recovery she is still a special friend. A heartfelt thanks also to Jen Kobenstein from Madison Wisconsin USA for her words of encouragement when she read early drafts.

Last and not least I want to thank Mike Smith who has also contributed in many ways to this book. When Mike and I first met I do not think either of us realised what we were to spark of in each other. We are now close friends and still work together regularly, together we hold a dream that one-day recovery shall become the norm in mental health and Mike continues to work tirelessly towards this goal.

Finally to all those I have not mentioned above especially Ian Murray (got you) thank you very much you know whom you are.

Ron Coleman

D1101678

DEDICATION

To all those who have died before recovery became a reality
If there is an after-life may you find recovery and healing there.
To all those who still await recovery it is yours for the taking

.

RECOVERY AN ALIEN CONCEPT?

BY

RON COLEMAN

FOREWORD

Mental illness, madness or whatever you choose to call it has been a preoccupation of mine from the first day that I walked or rather was dragged into the Royal Free psychiatric unit in London. That was the day that a psychiatrist who had known me for less than one hour concluded that I was suffering from a mental illness called schizophrenia. This one-hour meeting changed my whole life. Admittedly my life up to this meeting had not been the most enjoyable life on record indeed it had been a fairly lonely and unhappy existence.

A few months as an in-patient changed all that, far from being lonely and unhappy, I became totally isolated and depressed. For the next ten years my life was to be controlled by the psychiatric system, in that time my brother in law on meeting me for the first time thought; "what the hell is that"? He was referring to the pitiful sight that I had become when he met me five years after my admission into hospital. He later told me he wanted to shoot me to put me out of my misery.

The psychiatric system far from being a sanctuary and a system of healing became for me like for so many others a system of fear and continuation of illness. Like so many others recovery was a process that I did not encounter within the system, indeed I can honestly say that it was not until I left the system that the recovery process really got underway in my life.

It was as if the system had no expectation of me recovering, instead the emphasis was on maintenance. I am not saying that those who worked in the system did not care for me, they did they clothed me, fed me, housed me and ensured that I took my medication. What they did not do was consider the possibility that I could return to being a person not as I once was but the person that I could become perhaps even more than I once was. Indeed I could become Ron Coleman.

Within the pages of this book I hope to explore with you the possibility that recovery can be a reality not just for the lucky one or two but for the great majority of those who enter the psychiatric system.

In this new millennium, there is a need to reflect on the past and to learn the lessons of history. Recovery an Alien Concept is an attempt to do just this, it is not an academic book I hope, though students may find it useful. Rather it is an exploration of recovery, hopefully a guidebook and perhaps a book that will encourage professionals, clients and carers to begin their own personal journeys towards recovery.

In this the second edition of this book I have revisited my own journey and expanded on much of my thinking about self, the medical model and the situation that users and professionals are about to find themselves in with the introduction of compulsory treatment orders that will deny people their freedom even in their own communities.

I have also indulged myself by looking at how systems and practice might come together to create a whole systems approach. I would like to put on record once again the help that John Jenkins has given me in thinking through this section.

This edition written in the spring and summer of 2004 has also taken into account the constructive criticisms made about the first edition.

I hope that those who read this book will find in its pages not only criticism of the present system, the pain of those who the system has failed; but also the hope for the future, the inspiration of those who have recovered, and finally a desire to make recovery a reality in the this millennium.

Ron Coleman 2004.

INTRODUCTION

A PERSONAL ACCOUNT

The making of a schizophrenic

There is a joke that many service users know that goes like this. What is the difference between God and a psychiatrist? Answer, God does not think he is a psychiatrist. There is another major difference between God and a psychiatrist whereas it took God six days to create the world a psychiatrist can change a person's world in a little under an hour.

If the journey to recovery is for many a difficult one, it is often the case that the journey to illness is far too easy. My own journey to illness far from being a series of biological or chemical events was in simple words the culmination of personal life events that I had never dealt with.

Before I tell my story I would like to point out that my story is not that much different from the millions of others, world-wide who have been in, or are still in the psychiatric system. I am no braver or cleverer than most others in the system neither am I somehow different, my story is an ordinary one and should be treated as such.

Those of you who read the foreword know that a doctor in London diagnosed me as having schizophrenia if you did not know this then you have not read the foreword and should do so now. My story does not start with an enforced meeting with a psychiatrist in 1982 it starts a long time before this. It starts in actual fact in 1969 with a young boy's desire to become a Roman Catholic priest. I was that young boy and though people laugh now when I tell them I wanted to be a priest at the age of eleven I was smitten by the thought.

I was brought up in a working class, Scottish, Irish, Roman Catholic family and like many boys my age I went through my religious phase in my eleventh year of life. I went to see our parish priest and told him that I wanted to become a priest. Our parish priest at this time was getting on in years and was one of the old school, having said more masses in Latin than in English. He was also without doubt a man of God who saw himself as a shepherd and we mere mortals as his flock. When one among his flock stated they wanted to become a priest, he took them seriously. He took my desire to become a priest seriously and once a week I met with him and two other boys who had also stated a desire to enter the priesthood. In these weekly meeting we would discuss further the teachings of the church, the role of the priest and whether we thought our calling to the priesthood was real. After one such discussion one of the boys stopped coming as he felt he was not being called but was trying to please his family. The two of us that remained were undeterred and continued on with our instruction, fully committed to the idea that some day we would become priests.

These were happy days for me, I was preparing to serve God and I had all the enthusiasm an eleven-year old could muster for my coming tasks. The day that changed my life started the same as any other I went to school and after school I headed for the chapel house for instruction. The housekeeper answered the door, she was near to tears as she told us our parish priest had taken seriously ill earlier in the day, he survived this illness but he never returned to our parish. (I often wonder what would have happened had he never became ill. Would I now be a priest?) Shortly after this happened a new parish priest arrived, (I will call him Adrian) at first everything was business as usual and I soon relaxed into my normal routine. The next three months went by without incident as far as I was concerned though I noticed that a lot of the altar boys were leaving service before they normally would.

I was very quickly to find the reason why when after Mass one day Father Adrian asked me to come and see him in the vestry, I sauntered over without any thought as to why he wanted to see me after all he was a priest. When I arrived at the vestry Father Adrian asked me to sit down it was at this point that things started to change. He started by asking me if I had any sins that I needed to confess, when I said I did not he called me a liar and said that he needed to pray for me so that I would be forgiven. He knelt beside me and started praying aloud he was saying something about me leading him into sin and that I was evil. As he continued to pray he started moaning and groaning, I was aware that his hand was slowly moving up my leg this went on until he was touching my penis. As this continued I was aware of becoming a spectator in what was happening to me. I became aware of other things around me like the candles that were burning too brightly and his purple vestments were if anything even more purple than usual. I was there but not there those who have been abused will know what I mean, much later in my life I discovered that this is called dissociation and it is the most common form of self-preservation of those who are abused. At the time it did not feel much of a defence to me for inside I screamed at him to stop I also screamed at God for protection but either God was deaf or I never screamed loud enough because he never defended me. When it was over Adrian told me that no one would believe me if I told them what had happened. I left the vestry in a daze and never told anyone what happened that day or the many other days that it was to continue for.

I was trapped for a while within this cycle of abuse, after all who would believe me? Adrian was a priest he stood between people and God, he represented Christ on earth, the forgiver of sins, the good shepherd. I was an eleven-year old boy, a dreamer and to say anything would brand me a liar. My relationship with this God that I thought I believed in was over. The abuse continued for a few months until I found from somewhere the strength to turn my back fully on the church and with it God. My spiritual and religious phase was over. Time has taught me that this is the pattern with abusers that they are often in positions of trust in the community and they use this position to ply their evil trade in misery and pain. Experience has taught me that the failure to deal with abuse means that the abuse will stay with you throughout your life and in many ways shape your life in terms of future relationships. This is especially true when it comes to trusting friends or life partners. This event more than any other was to shape my life or should I say illness.

If this was the only traumatic life event that I was to go through I believe that I would have survived it and got on and led a fairly normal life. As is often the case it was when I thought that I had turned a corner that life dealt me its foulest hand. As I grew up into adulthood I put the abuse behind me or so I thought and got on with the business of living, it was while I was getting on with life that I met Annabelle. I met her one Saturday night in the pub after I had been playing rugby, when I saw her I knew what love at first sight meant. Being psychotic has nothing on being in love, love is without question the true psychotic experience. Annabelle was an artist, sculpture was her main medium though also she painted and did sketching. In the short time that we were together she taught me many things, she taught me what love was, how to make love and most importantly how to love life. She also taught me to appreciate the arts such as classical music, opera and theatre. With her I began to discover a spiritual dimension to my life though I hasten to add that this was not a religious thing.

Our relationship developed quickly from the torrid passion of new lovers to the passion that consumes those who are indeed soul mates. We spent as much time as we could in each other's company often we would sit up through the night talking and planning as couples do. We were planning our life together; this was normality at its best. But like all normality madness was lurking waiting its chance to pounce and consume us and then one day it did.

Like the day I met Annabelle the day our relationship ended was a Saturday, I had been playing rugby and went home with something for both of us to eat. When I got in I called to Annabelle asking her if she wanted tea or coffee, she didn't reply. I went into the living room and she was lying on the coach I asked her again and still got no reply I gave her a shake but she would not wake up. I rushed out of the house to a neighbour and asked them to phone an ambulance. They rushed her to hospital and put her on a life support machine she did not make it and three days later she was pronounced dead. Annabelle had taken her own life I never really found out why but I know that I blamed myself, I don't know why I blamed myself though it was to be many years before I stopped doing so.

When she died a large slice of me died also, I swore that never again would I get emotionally involved with anyone. Like many others I suppressed all of my emotions about Annabelle and her death. I continued on with a semblance of existence that others called life. Like the abuse I choose to pretend it never happened and like the abuse my feelings of grief and loss and hatred of the world festered inside growing and growing waiting for their chance to devour me.

The time came for my emotions to overcome me when I had an accident on the rugby pitch that put me out of the game forever. Barely weeks had passed since I was discharged from hospital (still on crutches) when I heard a voice for the first time. I was in my office waiting for the computer to deliver the results of some data I had inputted when a voice behind me said that I had done it wrong. I looked behind me but there was nobody there. I stopped what I was doing immediately, went to the pub and got drunk, I remember thinking that I was stressed and needed a break.

Within a short six-month period the voice had been joined by other voices that spent most of the day screaming at me. I could not focus on my work and the only relief I got was when I had drunk myself into oblivion. Eventually my boss told me I had four weeks to get my act together. Four weeks later I was out of work, losing my home and on my way (though I didn't know it then) to my first encounter with the psychiatric services. In double quick time I became a pitiful sight with an unkempt beard, more often than not dirty clothes and more and more frequently drunk rather than sober.

Eventually I could not take any more and I phoned the Samaritans and after much talking went to see my GP. He ended the consultation with the words "I am going to arrange for you to see a specialist" fine I thought that will take a while, what a surprise I was in for. He took me out of his consulting room and asked me to wait in a small side room in the surgery a few minutes later he returned with a nurse who he told me was going to look after me while he arranged an appointment with the specialist. The only thing I remember about that wait with the nurse was how little she spoke it was as if she was frightened to be in the same room as me.

My short wait ended some three hours later when the GP returned with another man it turned out that this man was the specialist that the GP had contacted. The specialist introduced himself and told me that he was a doctor and that he had come to see me since my GP was concerned about me. It was here that I went through my very first one-hour present state examination, after the interview the psychiatrist told me I was ill and it would be better if I came into hospital for a short time. I told him where to shove his hospital and fled the surgery, three days later I was dragged into the Royal Free hospital where I once again was subjected to the psychiatric interview with the conclusion that I was suffering from schizophrenia.

The psychiatrist there told me that if I took medication then my voices and other symptoms would be eradicated and I would get better. He told me that the medication took about two weeks to work and in no time at all I would be back to something like my old self, he was wrong. Two weeks went by and if anything I was worse not better so I stopped taking the medication and decided to leave. This was when I discovered the real power of the system I was put on a section two of the mental health act, which held me for up to twenty-eight days against my will. A section three this is a treatment order, which allowed them not only to detain me but also to medicate me forcibly if necessary, followed the section two in quick time. This became my new way of life a constant round of illness with short periods of respite (not wellness) in the community.

Over the next ten years I was to spend six of them as an in-patient almost all of them on a section three. In this time I had nearly forty sessions of ECT, tried nearly every neuroleptic on the market and was denied psychological interventions on numerous occasions. Despite the most vigorous of treatment regimes the voices I heard remained as virulent as ever, medication gave me no respite and eventually the volume of medication I was taking was so high that I became little better than a zombie who viewed life through a legalised drug induced smog.

The system did teach me things the main one being how to be a good schizophrenic, I do believe that we learn much about how to be mentally ill in the system. Ten years were to pass before I found a way out the system by then they (the system) had created a perfect schizophrenic. Now on to the recovery journey.

The stepping-stones to recovery

Any recovery journey has a beginning, and for me the beginning was my meeting with Lindsay Cooke my support worker, it was her who encouraged me to go to the hearing voices self-help group in Manchester at the start of 1991. It was her not me who believed that a self-help group would benefit me. It was her who saw beneath my madness and into my potential, it was her faith in me that kick started my recovery and it is to her that I owe an enormous debt.

There are other essentials required for a journey to be successful; one of these is the ability to be able to navigate to your desired destination. In this I was fortunate not to have one navigator but many. In this section I will mention only five of them. The first is Anne Walton a fellow voice hearer who at my very first hearing voices group asked me if I heard voices and when I replied that I did told me that they were real. It does not sound much but that one sentence has been a compass for me showing me the direction I needed to travel and underpinning my belief in the recovery process.

The second is Mike Grierson; Mike was the person who navigated me through my first contact both with my voices and with society. He encouraged me to go out and socialise with people who had nothing to do the psychiatric system. He also took me to places like the cinema and classical concerts which reawakened my love for the arts. Mike was not only my social navigator he was also one of the people who helped me to focus on my voices in a way that allowed me to explore my experience.

The third and fourth are Terry McLaughlin and Julie Downs, Terry and Julie were my navigators back to normality, they rekindled my interest in politics and took me into their family without reservation. It was with Terry that I developed much of my early thinking around training and mental health. With Julie as a co-worker I started to develop training packages, which we used to explore the world of mental health.

My fifth person is Paul Baker another of my navigators on the road to recovery, Paul who brought the hearing voices network to the United Kingdom encouraged me to become involved in the network, then when the time was right handed over the development of voices groups to me. To all of my navigators Anne, Mike, Terry, Julie and Paul I owe my sanity.

Navigators require a map or a plan from which to navigate, and I have been fortunate for the people who were my mapmakers, Patsy Hage, Marius Romme and Sandra Escher. I do not believe that these three fully understand what they have done. Little did Patsy know when she read the book by Julian Jaynes that the questions this would make her ask were going to affect so many people indeed It is because of her questions that the Hearing Voices Network and Resonance and other networks throughout the world exist today. Whether she wants it or not she has a premier place in the history of the hearing voices movement.

Sandra Escher is without doubt the person who made sure that ordinary people could understand the maps that were being made. Her ability to put across the message in language that is accessible to everyone has meant that their work has not remained in the world of academia but has been used by voice hearers from the very beginning. Sandra and Patsy have played a very important part in my recovery.

The final map maker is Marius Romme, Marius who in his own words is a
Traditional psychiatrist, is without doubt one of the greatest map makers who
it has been my good fortune to know. When he listened to Patsy Hage and
explored what she was saying it was then in my opinion he stopped being a
traditional psychiatrist. When he asserted in public for the first time that
hearing voices was a normal experience and that voice hearing was not to be
feared he stopped being a traditional psychiatrist. When he continued his work
despite being ridiculed and criticised by his peers he stopped being a traditional
psychiatrist and in my opinion became a great psychiatrist.

To Patsy Sandra and Marius I only owe one thing and that is my life.

Up to this point I have mentioned nine people who have been participants in one
way or another in my recovery journey and therein lies the first

stepping stone to recovery; people.

If I were to name all the people who have played a part in my recovery the list would be massive. The other thing about this list would be the fact that the majority on it would not be professionals. One of my fundamental beliefs about recovery is the premise that recovery cannot and does not happen in isolation. Nor can it happen if all our relationships are based on a professional and client interaction. Recovery is by definition wholeness and no one can be whole if they are isolated from the society, in which they live and work.

For many years I had argued that there is no such thing as mental illness this has lead me into some interesting debates with people over the last few years. One of these debates was with Marius Romme, during this discussion it became clear, that Marius was not arguing a case for biological illness, what he in fact was saying was that illness could be expressed as a persons inability to function in society. This I can accept as it means that recovery is no longer a gift from doctors but the responsibility of us all.

This raises the question of whether society is prepared to take any kind of
responsibility for the recovery of people with mental health problems. I am of the opinion that it will not, for in our sophisticated culture we too have bought into the notion of a biological explanation for mental health. I suppose that my expectations of society might appear to be too high, but that must be seen in the context of those societies that do accept responsibility for those amongst them who become mad.

For Example, in the Aboriginal Culture when someone goes mad the whole tribe comes together to discuss what the tribe has done to cause the person to be mad. Can you imagine this happening in our culture? I think not. When someone goes mad in our culture it is off to hospital with him or her. It is not a gathering of the local community that gets together to decide what is wrong with the community. It is a ward round made up of so called experts who get together often without the person concerned being present who decide both what is wrong with the client and how it will be treated. This scenario, alas all to familiar, does not hold out much chance of recovery for the client. It is an impersonal rather than a person centred way of approaching the problem. Within this scenario recovery is objective not subjective and the person is no longer a real factor in the process.

If people are the building bricks of recovery then the cornerstone must be self. I believe without reservation that one of the biggest hurdles we face on our journey to recovery is our relationship with self. Recovery requires self-confidence, self-esteem, self-awareness and self-acceptance without this recovery is not just impossible it is not worth it.

We must become confident in our own abilities to change our lives; we must give up being reliant on others doing everything for us. We need to start doing these things for ourselves. We must have the confidence to give up being ill so that we can start being recovered. We must work at raising our self- esteem by becoming citizens within our own communities despite our communities if need be. We are valued members of our societies and we must recognise our value. We need to recognise our own faults the system may have created our diagnoses, but often it is ourselves who reinforce it. We need to be aware of our learned behaviours this should be part of our old lives. We need to change those behaviours that still trap us in our roles as patients. We need to accept and be proud of who and what we are, I can honestly say my name is Ron Coleman and I am psychotic and proud. This is not a flippant statement this is a statement of fact.

I am convinced that when we grow confident about who and what we are; we can then be confident about who and what we might become. For me these four selfs; self-confidence, self-esteem, self-awareness and self-acceptance are the second stepping-stone on the road to recovery.

The third step is closely related to the second and it is rooted in our own status. I believe that we ourselves have a great deal of say in our own status. We can choose to remain victims of the system, we can choose to continue to feel sorry for ourselves, we can choose to remain the poor little ill person who requires twenty-four hour care from professionals. On the other-hand we can choose a different direction, we can choose to stop being victims and become victors, we can choose to stop feeling sorry for ourselves and start living again, we can choose to stop being the poor little ill person and start the journey of recovery. This for me is the third stepping stone; choice. When we thought of ourselves as ill it was easy to let others make our choices. The recovery road however demands that we not only make our own choices but that we take responsibility for all our choices good and bad. As we make choices we will make mistakes, we must learn to see the difference between making a mistake and having a relapse. For it is the easy option to go running back to the psychiatric system when we make mistakes. Rather than face our own weaknesses we fall into the trap of blaming our biology rather than our humanity. If people are the building blocks of recovery and self is the cornerstone then choice is the mortar that holds the bricks together.

There is one other stepping stone in the recovery process and that is ownership. Ownership is the key to recovery, we must learn to own our experiences whatever they are. Doctors cannot own our experiences, psychologists cannot own our experiences, nurses, social workers support workers, occupational therapists, psychotherapists, carers, and friends cannot own our experiences. Even our lovers cannot own our experiences. We must own our experiences. For it is only through owning the experience of madness can we own the recovery from madness.

The journey through madness is essentially an individual one, we can only share part of that journey with others, the greatest part of the journey is ours and ours alone. It is within ourselves that we will find the tools, strength and skills that we require to complete this journey for it is within ourselves that the journey itself takes place.

Recovery has become an alien concept, yet nothing I have talked about so far is based on rocket science, rather it is based on common sense, it is not anything new, it is merely a reiteration of a holistic view of life. We need to realise that sometimes we, all of us make things much more difficult than they need to be. It is almost as if we need life to be a rocket science that we never understand fully. We seem to spend much of our time making the complexities of living even more complex through our appliance of scientific objectivity rather than exploring our lives through the simple mechanism of personal subjectivity. The time has come to have a close encounter with an alien concept it is time for recovery.

Recovery is on the agenda, not clinical, not social recovery but personal recovery. The responsibility for recovery lies with us all, professionals, users, and carers, we can only achieve it by working together, we can only achieve it by talking and listening to each other. We can only achieve it through shifting the paradigm from one of biological reductionism to one of societal and personal development.

The work of Romme and Escher has started this paradigm shift it is up to all of us to continue this work until the shift has been made. Until we succeed people will still be locked away from society because they hear voices or see visions or have different beliefs. Until we succeed people will still be treated against their will, until we succeed society will still fear madness, until we succeed civilisation will remain uncivilised. Recovery is our common goal, it is achievable now, let us not lose the moment let us work together to make it happen, let us put our past differences behind us and let us go forward in this new millennium with new confidence. Let us go forward in this new millennium with a new concept of wellness; let us go forward in this new millennium under a united banner, let us go forward to recovery.

Let us at the same time be on our guard for even now the recovery idea is being bastardised by those who believe that maintenance is the same as recovery. In the year 2000 we saw the development of assertive outreach teams and the beginnings of the implementation of the national service framework. It is clear that the Government has decided to be hard nosed about the implementation insisting that assertive community treatment is at the centre of the plan. This is the case even though most professionals do not really understand the key principles that underpin the concept of assertive outreach.

If services were to adopt all of the principles of assertive community treatment as laid down by Stein and Teste then there would be the basis of a therapeutic alliance in which professional, service user and carer could work together. Should providers fail to adopt the principles of assertive community treatment and instead maintain their current obsession with compliance and ensuring that clients are compliant with their medication as being the core function of this service then there is no doubt in my mind that assertive community treatment will fail and will be renamed aggressive outreach. Instead of creating a safety net assertive outreach may end up like a trawler, which snares its net on a submarine and sinks without trace.

If assertive outreach is not to become the 21st Century Titanic of community mental health services then we must act now I am not arguing that we should get rid of assertive community treatment rather my argument is that we should ensure that where we set up assertive outreach teams then these teams understand the real principles of assertive community treatment and this in turn means that managers need to invest in high quality training for these teams.

There does however need to be some radical changes if assertive outreach is ever to become a service rooted in recovery the main one being the introduction of exit pathways from the service. At the time of writing assertive community treatment has effectively a no discharge policy and indeed is viewed by many professionals as a service for life.

Recovery an Alien Concept

The belief in recovery from serious mental illness is almost non existent in Western psychiatry, in its place we have adopted a concept of maintenance and social control for those we deem to be mentally ill. Does this mean that recovery is not possible for those classed as mentally ill? Or is it merely that we would have to put in too much effort into the present system in order to ensure a recovery process that would work? Or have we lost the knowledge and the skills that are required to work with people in a way that will enable recovery.

In our work Mike Smith and I have come to the conclusion that recovery is not only an alien concept for mental health professionals but also for carers and users of mental health services. We fundamentally believe that recovery is not only the desired outcome for service users but it is also possible for all service users to recover. Further to this we also believe that one of the biggest hurdles that a service user faces on their road to recovery is the psychiatric service that the user is in.

We have never doubted for a moment that the distress that service users suffer is real, nor do we question the validity of their experience, we accept fully the fact that people hear voices that no one else can or see things that others cannot see. Neither do we deny that some people have tactile or olfactory experiences that others cannot perceive or they have beliefs that are different and that are inconsistent with their peer groups. What we do not accept is the notion that people who continue to have these experiences are somehow biologically flawed and should hand their lives over to the psychiatric system often until they die.

Psychiatric services do little or nothing to dispel the myths that surround madness and even when they do attempt to do something it tends to be around educating people about a biological condition that they will at some point in the future find a way of curing. Psychiatrists have couched their profession in a scientific language that very few outside of the profession can understand, they have shrouded themselves within a discourse that alienates their clients and makes them sound as if they (the psychiatrists) understand the very secrets of the mind.

As Mike and I have developed our work I have come to the sad conclusion that in most services recovery is not even on the agenda. This is not only true in the United Kingdom but throughout the Western world and it is for this reason that I have decided to write this book. I do not pretend to have all the answers indeed I would claim to only have more questions but a start must be made and so let us begin our journey. Like any journey we must start at the beginning and the beginning of this journey is in defining what we mean when we talk about recovery.

What do we mean by recovery?

When we talk about recovery we must first decide what we mean by recovery, for example we often hear of doctors saying things like "John is making a good recovery". This sounds very positive but it tells us nothing about John, as we have no context in which to work in. What if John had just had two legs amputated then the doctors notion of recovery may well be that the operation has been a success and that the wounds are healing. John on the other hand may think that without his legs his life is over. If this is the case can we really say that John is making a good recovery, or is it the case that like most things in life recovery is a subjective rather than an objective concept.

The definition of recovery is one of the main differences that I have with many professionals involved in psychiatry. Too often the professionals view of recovery means little more than maintaining the patient in a "stable condition" regardless of issues such as adverse affects of medication or even the expressed wishes of the client. For myself recovery is a much more personal construct, indeed it is a construct, which in reality can only be, defined by the person himself or herself. The notion of a good recovery implies the concept of the existence of a bad recovery, which should be a contradiction too far. Unfortunately I do not believe that within the field of mental health it is a contradiction too far but the reality of many service users.

Let us return to John for a minute, he has taken the view that his life is in effect finished yet he will live. So what is he really saying? My opinion is that John is looking at the quality of his life rather than the fact that his wounds are healing, for John life without legs is not a viable proposition at this time. This may well change in time as alternatives are pointed out to him, but at this point in his journey there is no way that John would consider himself to have recovered. Indeed he may never consider himself as recovered, but he will be discharged from hospital and eventually from outpatients to all intention purposes recovered.

I would argue that the same is true in mental health, in that psychiatrists will measure recovery, using methods that mean very little to the client. A good example of this is the continual use of the symptoms rating scale as an outcome measure, this scale will tell us things like whether the person is still hearing voices but it will not tell us if the person can now cope with the voices. Even the use of quality of life scales, tells us very little about whether the person feels they have recovered or not.

Even at the beginning of our quest to understand the recovery process, we face our first obstacle that is, defining the recovery process. The two most common types of recovery that are talked about within the mental health system are clinical recovery and social recovery. The first question we must answer is what do these two models of recovery really tell us about our practice when they are applied to a recovery process.

Clinical Recovery

Clinical recovery as the term implies means the absence of symptoms either due to them being eradicated by treatment and the person being cured, or the absence of symptoms because the treatment is suppressing or controlling them.
It does not matter which of these definitions you use as much as the theory that underpins them. The essential of clinical recovery is that the recovery process occurs because of the effectiveness of the clinical treatment.

At first it somewhat surprised me then that when I was reading "Essential Psychiatry" edited by N. Rose as part of my research for this book that the word recovery was not to be found within the index. I must confess though that when I thought it through by looking at those I knew who were in the system, the sense of surprise faded and was replaced by that of foreboding. Undeterred I searched other books with the same results, no mention of recovery. So is there a relationship between clinical recovery and recovery? Or is clinical recovery only a form of language that psychiatrists have picked up from their medical colleagues in other disciplines?

Even where the word recovery is discussed, by psychiatrists (like Dick Warner) it tends to be viewed in a theoretical or an historical setting rather than in a practical setting. Indeed in the 1990's what is often discussed when deciding the pathway for a client is an abstract notion of recovery called outcomes. The psychiatric trade has in effect created a language that meets the professionals, rather than the service users needs.

Spot the Difference.

There are now two words that we have to define in order to explore what clinical recovery really means and more importantly what value clinical recovery has for service users, These are recovery and outcomes.

The concise Oxford dictionary offers us various definitions of recovery these are:

1   *Regain possession or use or control of, acquire or find (out) again, reclaim.*
2   *Secure by legal process.*
3   *Retrieve, make up for, cease to feel effects of.*
4   *Hence ~ able.*
5   *Come or bring back to consciousness, health or Normal State or position.*

For our purposes of medicine the definition should be the one that takes health and normal state as its core statement. Is this the definition that is practised within the current psychiatric service? When we look at the definition of outcome in the dictionary, it offers only three words. These are:

1   *Result, visible effect.*

I would argue that psychiatry is based on an abstract notion of results and visible effects rather than on any meaningful definition of recovery. Gowers described the use of the word outcome in the

English language as " one of the words specially liable to slovenly use..."

The use of an outcome, biased approach to mental health carries with it the risk of alienating the client from the recovery process through the limited measures used to determine outcomes. Which will in turn limit the interventions used, to those interventions that will achieve the predetermined outcomes desired by the professional.

The use of outcome rather than recovery measures has major benefits to professionals; one of these is that it allows professionals within mental health to avoid the obvious contradiction that would have to be faced about clinical recovery. This is that if recovery is based on the clinical effectiveness of the treatment and clinical recovery equates with wellness, it would also seem that the opposite is true that if someone did not clinically recover then they would remain unwell. This surely also means that the treatment has been ineffective, in layman's terms it has not worked.

Measuring the outcome rather than recovery makes sense for professional's as the possibility for bad results or outcomes is as readily available as the possibility of good results or outcomes. If on the other hand we were to measure recovery it would become distinctly uncomfortable for professionals as we do not hear much said about bad recovery indeed bad recovery does not exist you either recover or you do not. Even the use of partial recovery is not something that lends itself to the debate, or can a person be a bit of a schizophrenic?

One can argue therefore that outcomes are a way of sanitising the non-recovery process rather than measuring a recovery process. The need to sanitise the non-recovery process can be clearly rooted in the psychiatrist's need to use a medical frame of reference as a means to understand mental distress. It is clear that within the medical model there is little or no notion of recovery for those with conditions such as schizophrenia. Indeed the emphasis when working with people described as having enduring mental illness is always on maintenance, i.e. preventing relapse. This lays at the heart of clinical recovery not the possibility of cure but the probability of relapse. This probability model of care and treatment is now the most commonly used model we may dress it up in fancy titles such as assertive outreach or continuing needs services but essentially it is a probability methodology that we operate. This by definition means that professionals must utilise a defensive practise method thereby rejecting even the possibility of recovery.

Defensive practise.

The use of defensive practise, indeed the notion of defensive practise has at its foundation not any concept of clinical governance or beneficial practise for the client but the almost paranoid fears of professionals of being held legally accountable if anything goes wrong. During a trip to the USA I asked an American psychiatrist why he could on the one hand write and talk so radically about schizophrenia and its social and economic causes yet use so much medication on his clients. His reply was simple he lived in constant fear of litigation from patients or their families if anything went wrong. He told me that his best defence if anything went wrong was to prove in court that he had been actively treating his client with drugs as laid down by the American Psychiatric Association. This rationale also underpins much of the psychiatric professions' attitudes in the United Kingdom. In the UK when a psychiatrist faces charges of negligence his only defence is to call members of his peer group to say they would have acted in the same way in the same circumstances. I am of the opinion that this means that the law is not interested in whether it was the right or wrong thing to do but whether it is what other doctors would have done.

The consequence of this narrow view of right and wrong is that psychiatrists are safer when they continue to do only the done thing. This in turn means that they will not take risks of any kind not out of any fear for the client but pure and simply from the fear of what might happen to them. This reduces the tool-kit at the disposal of the doctor down to the "safe" options of medication ECT or radical surgery. This begs the question of how effective then are the treatment tools available to doctors in terms of achieving recovery.

Medication.

Most psychiatric doctors appear to be wedded to the idea that they must treat everyone with medication and that it is only through the use of medication that people recover. The evidence for this view appears to be based on research carried out using moneys supplied by the pharmaceutical industry. I am constantly amazed when I attend conferences at the number of research papers available from drug companies that prove how effective their products are in the treatment of conditions like schizophrenia. My amazement stems not only from the volume of papers but from the fact that if the claims contained within these papers were true then why are such a high number of people who are diagnosed as having schizophrenia still actively psychotic despite the medication.

I have never disputed the fact that for some people medication has produced life changing and life saving results and for these people the use of medication has without doubt had great benefits. Indeed research has shown that fully 33% of people using neuroleptic medication recover to such an extent that they will no longer require psychiatric services. This however, does not change the fact that for 66% of people the medication regime works either in a very limited way or not at all. In my opinion it is both dangerous and foolish to see medication as anything more than a short-term strategy when dealing with peoples mental health problems, there are a number of reasons that I take this position though I intend to explore only a few of these within this book.

The long-term effects of psychotropic medication are not fully known especially the so-called atypical neuroleptics or the new anti-depressants such as prozac. What we do know about the (so-called) side effects of medication should be enough in my estimation to make psychiatrists rethink the use of this type of treatment as a long-term strategy. We know that at least one person a week dies as a direct result of neuroleptic medication (National Mind Figures). We know that prozac contrary to the manufactures claim is addictive. We know that for many clients they perceive the "side-effects" of medication, as being worse than the symptoms that are being treated.

Medics conveniently ignore this knowledge when they are talking to clients about the treatment they are receiving. Other factors, which have also been conveniently ignored, are issues such as personality changes, which can occur as a direct result of medication. A good example of this is the number of people who have become aggressive and violent after starting to use prozac. Add to this the incidence of people contracting neurological problems such as tardive dyskensia after prolonged use of neuroleptics, and it is no wonder that many of us consider psychiatry to be in a constant state of crisis. Do not get me wrong I for one would have liked nothing better than to have gone to hospital for a couple of weeks, taken my medication and been discharged to all intention purposes well. This was not my experience for like many others no matter what medication I was given my condition did not improve in any meaningful way. Despite this I have never had a problem with the use of medication as a treatment for those with mental health problems, I do have a problem with the misuse of medication and its continuing usage even when there are no benefits to the client.

It is the constant misuse of medication that I cannot understand. If medication does not help a particular individual in anyway, how can its continued use be justified? The answer that the psychiatrist has to this question is to declare that it is not the medication that is failing the client but the client that is failing the medication. It is common within psychiatry to describe someone who is not responding to medication as being drug resistant even when they get adverse affects of the drug.

Rather than say a drug is not working they find it easier to blame the persons own biology or physiology for the ineffectiveness of the treatment. The professional response to this type of client beggars belief, many of these clients are subjected to ever increasing dosages of medication and the practise of polypharmacy amongst this group is staggering.

The more I have read about medication and how it works the more I have become convinced that a client does not need to be tried on every drug within a grouping that is available. Indeed I would now argue that in the case of neuroleptics there are only two types available typical and atypical and if a person is tried on one of each and they fail then surely there is no point in continuing to try other drugs within the same group. Indeed the only argument that can be even remotely valid is the need to change medication that is working, in order to decrease the adverse effects a person may be getting.

There is very little in common between the above type of medication regime and a truly person centred approach to recovery. It is this absence of a person centred approach that condemns the medication approach most. Medication is not worked out on an individual basis for the individual but rather on macro factors worked out by the pharmaceutical industry based on clinical trials using poor methodology. This type of statement cannot be made if it cannot be fully justified, and it is my intention therefore to explore the reasons I have made this statement in the chapter on methodology.
One of my friends Phil Thomas who is a consultant psychiatrist often talks about the two levels of drug intervention. The first level is an

intervention based on the use of small doses of drugs especially when using anti-psychotics he calls this the therapeutic dosage. The second level of intervention is when a high dosage of drugs is used he calls this social control. In his book The Dialectics Of Schizophrenia he writes:

"Concern about the use of high doses of neuroleptic medication has focused on two areas in particular. Many psychiatrists and psychiatric nurses working in in-patient units feel that the conditions found in these units contribute to the need to use high doses of medication"

He then points out that in his experience junior doctors were called out more frequently to write up medication when there were fewer staff on duty. What this is pointing to is the relationship between environment and how clients respond or feel. This should not come as any surprise, but it appears that for many professionals the correlation between environment and symptoms somehow eludes them. The next area of concern that Thomas writes about is the treatment of young black men he writes:

"The second worry concerns the use of high doses of medication in particular groups, particularly young Afro-Caribbean men. This has almost certainly contributed to the sudden death of a number of young black men over the last ten years".

Thomas then concludes that an enquiry (Special Hospital Service Authority 1993) suggests that the reason for the high dosage of drugs in this group was a reflection of:

".....crude stereo-types that black men were potentially dangerous. White health professionals often find it difficult to conceal the fact that they perceive young black men as 'dangerous' or 'violent' and it is for this reason that this group is liable to receive higher doses of neuroleptic medication". (Thomas 1997)

It is not surprising therefore that many black people that I know who have used our services would describe white professionals who are treating them as "dangerous" or "violent". In any other area of our lives such as in employment or education treating black people in this way would be seen as racial discrimination. The only other grouping who acts in the same way towards black people with the same impunity are the police. Perhaps this is one more piece of evidence that psychiatry is often used within our society as an agency of the state, as enforcers of social control.

The use of medication as a means of social control is nothing new; we have often in history attempted to deal with social problems using chemical solutions. Perhaps the greatest mess we have ever made in this Country involved the use of valium, which was given to tens of thousands mainly women who were finding it difficult to cope with their home environment. The drug never dealt with the problems of their home lives what it did do however was to create tens of thousands of drug addicts.
These women were turned into addicts not through choice but through the short sightedness of the medical establishment and the greed of the drug companies. This disaster is in the process of repeating itself as we now find the new drug prozac being prescribed for many of the same reasons as valium was prescribed. Despite assurances from the manufacturers of the drug that it is not addictive there have already been cases of addiction reported and no doubt in time we will pay the same high price for our failure to learn the lessons of history.

Another common belief about medication is that people who stop their medication will always relapse. This view seems to be supported by research such as that carried out by Dencker et al (1980) which found that 50% of their non-complaint client group symptoms came back within six months and after twelve months the relapse rate rose to 80%. Though this is a very high relapse rate the study does not tell us anything about the quality of life for the client group after their symptoms re-appeared. There is also the fact that 20% of the client group had no reoccurrence of symptoms, yet our system would still insist that they remain on their medication over a long period. For this 20% the evidence clearly shows that the medication is not needed though in many Countries they may well be forced to take medication even in the community through the systems use of mental health laws. If 20% of people in our prison system were being held for crimes they did not commit we would have an international outcry about the miscarriage of justice being perpetrated by the state. The reason I have used this study is that it gives one of the highest relapse rates. Other studies have relapse rates that are much lower Johnson (1979) found a 60% relapse rate amongst those who stopped taking their medication in his study. In trials where placebos were used Pasamanick et al 1964 found that 45% of the group on placebos relapsed over an eighteen month period whilst Hirsch et al found that 50% of the group on placebos relapsed over a nine month period.

These results are I believe a damming indictment on the psychiatric system, as they as they put in doubt the value of concentrating on a medication strategy in the treatment of those who have been labelled as seriously mentally ill. The fact that in one of the studies (Pasamanick et al 1964) 65% of patients on placebo medication, that is, not on medication did not relapse must at the very least generate doubt in the present understanding of the causes of the mental distress in this case the dopemine theory. If we extrapolated this to figures rather than percentages, it would mean that out of one thousand people on neuroleptic medication six hundred and fifty would find the same benefits from taking a placebo as they would from taking the real thing. This would also be without any of the adverse effects caused by the use of neuroleptics. These figures also point to the inherent dangers in basing practice on a theory that has not been proven.

Stopping Medication A Dangerous Dilemma

For many the dilemma they face when stopping medication has less to do with relapse and more to do with the consequences of withdrawal from medication
Breggin in his classic book Toxic Psychiatry writes:

"Because of the withdrawal problems, patients should try to come off the medications while receiving emotional and social support from others and with supervision by someone familiar with the process. It should be understood that withdrawal symptoms may encourage the doctor and the patient alike to resume the drug prematurely, when what the patient really needs is time to recover from the drug"

In this extract Breggin is spelling out clearly something that many of us have speculated about for a long time and that is the addictive qualities of psychotropic medication in general and neuroleptic medication in particular. How often do doctors tell their clients that the effects they feel when they stop their medication is due to relapse rather than any thing to do with the withdrawal from the drug or drugs? At worst this is another example of the misinformation that professionals give users and carers and at best it shows how badly informed professionals are themselves. Either way it is a sad reflection on the ability of the psychiatric system to face up to its responsibilities to those who are subjected to its ministrations. For myself coming off neuroleptic medication was one of the most difficult things I have ever done. Even though I thought I understood what was going to happen to me when I stopped the medication (I was forced to go cold turkey because my psychiatrist would not support a reduction regime) nothing could prepare me for the reality of withdrawal.

Apart from sweating and shivering being sick and unable to sleep I heard even more voices than normal. I had visions, (something I had never experienced before) out of body experiences, (again new) and my thinking became muddled and confused. Add to this a developing paranoia and you can see that throughout the withdrawal process I was a prime candidate for hospital admission on the basis of relapse due to non-compliance. After four weeks of this my condition improved quickly and within another three weeks I was as near to being myself again as I had during the ten years I spent in the system. Reflecting back on this experience it is not something I would recommend. It would be better by far if those suffering from mental distress were given the right to opt for drug free alternatives and given the support they required to withdraw from the medication they are on in structured way.

The British Government however seems to think it knows what is best for those with mental health problems, in 1998 they started a review of mental health services saying that what they wanted was evidence based practice to ensure what they called good clinical governance. In almost the same breath the minister of state also said that for those deemed to be mentally ill non-compliance was not an option. In one sentence Government has declared the answer to something that has been the subject of heated debate for the last century by effectively stating that mental illness is a biological condition and that the way to treat it is to ensure compliance with medication. Indeed in the House of Commons in December 1998 the Minister of Health Frank Dobson declared he did not care what the experts thought what mattered is what he thought as he was the minister responsible. Words I fear that will come back to haunt him at a later date.

This unholy trilogy consisting of the Government the Royal College of Psychiatry and the Pharmaceutical Industry are relying on organisations such as SANE to spread its Gospel of enforced compliance. This unholy alliance is without doubt using all the resources at their disposal to undermine any alternative views on the way forward in treating those suffering from mental distress. Medication is not and never will be the solution that will cure all those suffering from mental health problems rather it will at best provide some relief for some people. To rely on medication is in my opinion folly that verges on negligence. If compliance is to ever become a reality then service providers must provide treatments that are based on client choice for if we make the choice to partake in a treatment regime then surely it follows that we will comply with that regime.

Electro-convulsive therapy

ECT is the second treatment within the psychiatrists tool-kit, as the doctor sees it ECT is a tool which he hopes to use to repair the damage that mental illness has caused the patient. Of all the treatment options open to the psychiatrist ECT is the most controversial in that it is at the centre of an ongoing acrimonious debate between users and psychiatrists. In the United Kingdom organisations such as ECT anonymous and the All Wales User and Survivor Network are calling for either the suspension of compulsory ECT or the banning of the treatment altogether.

The question we seek to answer in this book is: Does ECT as a treatment, have a place within the recovery process of people defined as having mental health problems? The starting point in answering this question is to understand what ECT is and what it does to people who are given ECT as treatment.

Electro-convulsive therapy is the passage of an electrical current through the brain in order to produce what are known as grand mal convulsions (epileptic fits). The theory is that the passage of electricity and the accompanying fit will stimulate brain activity in such a way that the person receiving the treatment will recover. Although it is primarily a treatment for depression it is used for clients with various diagnoses such as obsessive- compulsive disorder, hypermania and schizophrenia to name but a few.

The most common response to the question about how ECT works in terms of the recovery process is that no one knows how it works just that for some people it does work and it works in cases of severe depression really quickly. Indeed many professionals claim that without ECT a great number of people would die through self-neglect. It should also be pointed out that some people who have received ECT have made the same claim. Despite all of the claims made by those who are pro ECT I am now convinced that ECT should be banned and there should be no place for it within psychiatric practice. The reason I have taken this position on ECT is simple, and that is that as I have explored the facts surrounding ECT I have discovered that the establishment has been less than honest about what ECT does to the recipient. I will now lay out the facts I considered in coming to this conclusion.

In the year ending March 1990 106,000 treatments were administered in England alone, this means that about 17,000 people in that year received ECT. Lucy Johnston, in her book " Users and Abusers of Psychiatry" claims that the use of ECT is on the increase. She has concluded through her research that in England there are about 200,000 treatments administered each year with some hospitals using it up to seventeen times more often than others. This means that over 30,000 people a year receive courses of ECT. Most people who receive ECT will consent to this treatment by signing a form, though it can be given without consent to someone who is detained under the mental health act for treatment providing a second opinion concurs that the treatment is required.

I would argue that the notion of informed consent in the United Kingdom is a farce and that informed consent is rarely given, as the client is not provided with the information that is required to ensure that the consent is informed. Many of us now talk about the need for, real consent based on a full disclosure of information pertaining to the treatment.

For many years now psychiatrists have told patients that they did not know how ECT worked. This has not been the complete truth, indeed since the very early days of ECT supporters of the treatment have been clear that the main reason that ECT works is the damage it does to the brain.

The evidence that ECT damages the brain is well documented, research carried out in the 1940s and 1950s on cats, dogs and monkeys demonstrated clearly that animals subjected to ECT suffered scattered cell death and small brain haemorrhages after even small doses of ECT. Hans Hartelius was able to tell which cats had received ECT by microscopic examination of their brains. There is evidence from post-mortem examinations of similar cell death and brain haemorrhaging in humans who have had ECT.

In Peter Breggin's book Electroshock: Its Brain Disabling Effects (1979) Breggin points to other evidence that proves the damaging effects. He cites EEG studies, neuropsychological testing, brain scan studies and other clinical reports. These studies all show damage to the brain or psychological functioning that can only have been caused due to ECT. Breggin also notes the similarities between those who have had ECT and those suffering from head injury. At one point in Toxic Psychiatry he states:

"It is recognised in neurology that even mild head injury frequently results in lasting, debilitating problems, such as memory difficulties, deficiencies in focusing and maintaining concentration and loss of problem solving skills."

All of these post head injury problems can be clearly seen in people who have been subjected to ECT treatments. Surely this in itself is enough evidence to show that brain dysfunction is caused as a direct result of ECT. Max Fink one of the leading advocates of the use of ECT accepts as much. Fink accepts that both denial and euphoria experienced by those who have received ECT are directly linked to the amount of brain damage done by the treatment. Indeed Fink goes further when he claims that brain dysfunction is neither a "complication" nor a "side effect" but the "sin qua non of the mode of action. In other words Fink is relating the effectiveness of the recovery process to ability of ECT to cause brain damage. Fink is no radical campaigner trying to stop ECT he is the opposite. The reality of what he is advocating for those who have a mental health problem is simple brain damage is good for you.

The known adverse effects of ECT include death, brain damage, memory loss, seizures, suicide and personality changes all of which can also be detected in head injury patients. The decision our society must make seems clear is it justifiable to cause deliberate brain damage and call it making people better?

Psychosurgery.

The third tool available to the psychiatrist is that of psychosurgery. Though not often talked about it is still an option that is available to medics as a treatment. The practice of operating on peoples' brains is not something new; historically we can trace the practice back to the ancient Egyptians. Throughout history especially during times of war; surgeons (because of head wounds) related physical injury to the brain to changing emotional states.

Surgeons came to the conclusion that if head injury caused emotional change then deliberately cutting portions of the brain would also cause emotional change. Over 60 years ago researchers showed that certain nerve pathways between the limbic lobe and the frontal cortex were central to the control of mood. By dividing these nerve pathways they discovered that they could relieve high anxiety states and replace it with euphoric states.

Egos Moniz developed the operation that we now call a leucotomy in 1936. The operation was claimed to be an effective treatment of depression, obsessive- compulsive disorder and schizophrenia. This effectiveness is brought into question by the fact that the personality changes caused by the operation were in the words of Michael Haslam a supporter of psychosurgery;

"Personality disturbance was excessive, causing a somewhat fatuous and sociable mood which, while better than the previous state, still made such individuals a problem to themselves and their relatives".

Haslam goes on to explain that the techniques used in psychosurgery have advanced so that the dangers of adverse physical effects have become minimal, (*though the psychological and emotional changes are the same*). He does however acknowledge the real possibility of damage and justifies it saying;

"Obviously, no one wants to damage or remove any part of the body if its normal function can be restored without recourse to operation. It must be recognised, however, that in occasional cases normal function cannot be restored without recourse to operation, and the end justifies the procedure in such individuals".

This ends justifying the means is a common facet within psychiatry, it also emphasises one of the major bones of contention between the "psychiatrised" and the psychiatrist; that is the issue of who is in control of what happens.

There is no doubt that many people are surprised to learn that psychosurgery is still used and some express disbelief and anger that it happens at all. Like many others I assumed that surgery was the last resort treatment for violent schizophrenics, it was only when I started researching this form of surgery that I discovered how wrong I was.

In one survey of 85 patients who had been operated on the breakdown in terms of diagnoses was; depression 24, anxiety 20, obsessional compulsive states 19, violent behaviour 6, anorexia nervosa 5, intractable pain 4, schizophrenia 4, and self destructive behaviour 3. In actual fact only 13 people out of the 85 fitted in any way, shape or form with my pre-conception of the type who would be referred for psychosurgery.

"Essential Psychiatry" (Rose) which actually says little on the subject points out that psychosurgery is indicated only after prolonged use of conventional treatments has failed and is effective as a treatment for "intractable obsessional and depressive disorders". On the effectiveness of such surgery (pg191) it states;

"The usual result of the operation is a reduction in anxiety and tension. As a result treatments such as behaviour therapy that have previously been unsuccessful may now produce a remission in symptoms".

Despite early claims of success as a treatment that allowed people to leave hospital who may never have left without the operation especially those prone to violent mood changes, the role of psychosurgery as a tool for recovery is to say the least obscure if not unfounded.

At the present time there is an almost unanimous belief amongst professionals that not only should it be the treatment of last resort, but that it should be carried out only on selected patients after long deliberation. This is not a surprising belief since in the same section of the book the author observes that;

"There has been no controlled evaluation of psychosurgery, mainly because the nature of treatment renders such an investigation very difficult".

In light of the above statement and the emphasis being placed on evidence based practice founded on quality research I find it hard to understand why such a procedure is allowed to continue.

Damage Limitation

The clinical methods of treating people with mental health problems developed via medicine seem to have at their centre the concept of damage limitation rather than real recovery. This clinical approach to peoples' mental health is without doubt based on treating symptoms and behaviour as opposed to treating causes. Without doubt this approach is dehumanising in that it reduces the mind to the role of a by-product of the brain. The role of the patient is also clearly defined within this framework as that of a passive recipient whose only part in the process is to be compliant and not complain about their treatment.

This compliance is expected despite the fact that the adverse effects of all the treatments on offer are for many worse than the "illness" that is being treated. Indeed within mental health the emphasis on compliance is now so great that we have created specialist mental health teams whose role is to ensure compliance. In the United Kingdom the minister of state who is responsible for mental health repeatedly stated in 1998 that non-compliance was not an option for those deemed to have enduring mental health problems. Compliance does not increase the numbers of people who recover from mental health problems neither does coercion. If we are to succeed as a society in enabling people to find a route to recovery then we must stop reducing everything to peoples' biology.

There is a need to go beyond the limited tool-kit that is available to the biological psychiatrist in their quest to enable recovery. The psychiatrists tool-kit is for their patients' a double-edged sword. Though for some, biological and physical interventions appear to have some benefits we must ask ourselves the following question. Is the damage that these treatments can cause too high a price to pay for so called clinical recovery?

Social Recovery

Like clinical recovery our starting point in this chapter should be a working definition of social recovery. Unlike clinical recovery such a definition is difficult, due in no small measure to the differing contexts in which the word social is used within the field of mental health. For the purposes of this chapter the emphasis will be upon a behavioural construct of social recovery which views the recovery process as the persons ability or lack of to interact in a particular way within society. The reason for using this type of definition is that it is the one that most professionals seem to buy into when talking about social recovery. Warner in Recovery from Schizophrenia (1994) attempts to define social recovery as an outcome measure stating;

"If outcome is measured in terms of social functioning, the investigator may look at any combination of a range of features including the following: working ability, capacity to care for basic needs, abnormal behaviour causing distress to others, criminal activity, number of friends or sexual functioning".

This definition warrants close scrutiny so that we can test whether it is valid to define social recovery in terms of the above statement. Warner reduces the definition further when he argues that there is a need to "impose some consistency" when doing retrospective research on outcome studies and comes up with the following shortened definition;

"Economic and residential independence and low social disruption"

For myself the obvious flaw in the criteria that Warner is using to define social recovery is that many of the areas he uses to measure recovery are areas in our lives that we either have little or no control over. Warner himself recognises that in an ever changing, economic climate; individuals cannot control employment opportunities. The economic cycle of boom and bust lends itself to periods of high unemployment. It is evident that during times of low economic activity and high unemployment; therefore those in the community who have mental health problems are high in the priorities of employers who are looking to shed workers. It is equally evident that they are low in the priorities of those employers who are looking to take on workers.

Even in times of boom when the economy is vibrant the outlook for those who are, or have been in the psychiatric system and seeking employment is bleak. This is often due to the stigma that is prevalent in our society. Economic independence through real employment is for many service users nothing more than a pipe dream. In fact the reality facing most people termed as having enduring mental health problems is one of long-term economic dependence.

If those with long term problems spend most of their adult lives economically dependent on the state then we must by the above definition of social recovery reach the conclusion that for this group social recovery is not a possibility. One of the ways professionals who believe in this model of social recovery have squared this circle is to replace the emphasis on economic independence through real employment with a variety of alternatives based on the concept of meaningful activity. These alternatives normally include sheltered employment and supported employment, these options do create economic independence not for service users of course but for the professionals who are paid to operate such schemes. In his definition Warner talks about working ability, there is no doubt that service users want to work and have the ability to work what they face is the inability of society to accept their (the service users) abilities as valid.

Indeed throughout his definition of social recovery; Warner is by the nature of the research forced to use measures that are judgmental, value laden and smack of high morals. In fact in order to be socially recovered within this definition a service user would have to be more normal than normal.

Economic independence is a myth for many clients as is residential independence, and if these two factors are not in place then our ability to care for our basic needs must surely be disrupted. For the reality is simple the process of institutionalisation and stigmatisation that people who are or have been in the mental health system in itself causes a process that robs them of economic and residential independence. This creation of dependency that is part of the process of the mental health system in turn leads to the loss of clients' ability to care for their basic needs. It is somewhat ironic that one of the measures used in determining the level of a person's inability to function socially is only there because of the systems ability to create dysfunctional people.

The next part of the definition "abnormal behaviour causing distress to others" is once again subjective in construct and is therefore open to abuse through the interpretation of what is abnormal. Using subjective methodology professionals' cannot help but make value judgements and come to conclusions based on their own values, prejudices and baggage. Without doubt these values especially in the case of the medical profession do not necessarily reflect the values of society as a whole, rather they reflect the values of a privileged grouping within society.

If we were to apply the criteria of "abnormal behaviour causing distress to others" to professionals how would they fare? In 1999 one of my friends was detained against their will in a psychiatric hospital in England. The professional team who were looking after her decided at a review of her care that she should be denied any contact with family or friends. This was to include no visitors at all, no telephone calls and no writing or the receiving of mail. This decision was taken without consultation, my friend's advocate was not allowed to be present indeed during this enforced isolation he was not to be allowed to visit her. The family and friends of this woman were deeply distressed by the attitude and behaviour of the staff to both them and the woman. I for one would argue that apart from completely disregarding any human rights that a person has the team also through their abnormal behaviour caused distress to others. This is not an isolated case that I had to rack my brains for hours to find, indeed it would be all too easy to cite many others that confirm this view. Perhaps the most interesting thing to note is that following the logic of the definition of social recovery that we are exploring, in this area at least we can conclude that professionals have a long way to go to achieve their own recovery.

The remainder of the measures used by Warner, far from adding clarity to the concept of social recovery actually confuses the issue further. The emphasis that is placed on criminal activity creates the impression that one of the symptoms of mental illness is criminality. I find this idea abhorrent in the extreme in that it creates an unjustifiable stereotype of the behaviour patterns of those diagnosed as mentally ill. Organisations such as SANE have jumped on this imagined relationship between criminality and mental health making unsubstantiated claims about the relationship between violence especially homicide, mental illness and care in the community. SANE claim that there are over one hundred murders a year carried out by people with mental illnesses and that the number is increasing because of the failure of community care.

The reality is, as always, totally different research carried out by Taylor and Gunn (1999) on behalf of the Institute of Psychiatry discovered the following. In 1972 356 people were convicted of homicide. 130 of those convicted had a mental health problem, that is 36.5% in 1979 there were 480 people convicted of homicide. 121 of those convicted had mental health problems; that is 25%. In 1995 there were 522 people convicted of homicide. Only 60 of those convicted had mental health problems; that is 11.5%.

These figures fly in the face of claims made by the media and organisations such as SANE. This massive reduction in homicides carried out by people who have mental health problems does not change the fact that every time a homicide does occur that it is a tragedy for all those involved. What it does do however; is to put into perspective the scale of the problem.

There is no doubt that people with mental health problems do get involved in criminal activity, but since at least 25% of the population will at some point in their lives have a mental health problem, this should come as no great surprise. Once again the main problem in this area is one of perception. The antics of the media have done much in conditioning the general public in relating "mental illness" to criminality.

The real crime is the fact that most clinicians are using criminal activity as a measure of social recovery. This cannot but reinforce the belief that there is a definitive relationship between "mental illness" and crime. Using criminality as an indicator of social recovery is unjustifiable and should have no place in any modern mental health system.

Using the number of friends a person has, as a measure of social recovery is misleading to say the least in that it is based on a subjective notion of the number of friends a person should have. This number will be based on the individual professional's view of the number that is appropriate, in other words it is normally based on the number of friends that the professional has. This could be a major problem for users if the professional working with them is a popular person. The number of friends we have are influenced by other factors apart from our personality, these factors are varied and many for this book I will call them the "opportunity factors". Opportunity factors include such things as having enough income that allows you to go out and meet people, having links in the local area with people who share common interests with you and the level of medication a person has to take. I guess that the first question people might ask is how can the level of medication a person is on affect the amount of friends they have? For some the answer to this question is obvious, for many however, the relationship between social functioning and medication has not been established and therefore there is a lack of clarity around the issue. For myself I have no doubt that the amount and types of medication a person is on will affect their ability to function at a social level. The use of high levels of chemicals to control symptoms has meant that many clients spend much of their time in a drug-induced stupor with some spending up to twenty hours every day in bed.

The effects of medication in itself causes much of the social dysfunction and most certainly disables many clients to the extent that they will find it near impossible to start and maintain the social contacts that will lead to friendships forming.

The over prescribing of medication denies people opportunities to do many things that most in society take for granted. The last measure of social recovery that of sexual functioning is a classical example of the lack of understanding of the cause and effect relationship that goes on within the psychiatric system. If a client is spending twenty hours a day in bed and seeing the world through a drug created stupor then the chances are that his or her sex life is going to be limited. Even on small doses of medication there is no doubt that many clients sexual functioning is affected in a detrimental way. Once again the measure is flawed in that it does not take into account the effect that medication has on the person.

Indeed in every measure that Warner is using, the role of medication can adversely affect the outcome for the client and on this basis I would argue that the methodology that Warner has adopted to measure social recovery is fatally flawed. Indeed I would go further and argue that much of the work done around social recovery, is not about recovery at all rather it is about coping, making the best of things and accepting responsibility. This process may make life easier for all concerned when it is successful but it is not a process of recovery, it is what I would call a process of non-recovery that continues the client's dependence on the system.

Others use a similar methodology, Paul Carling in a position paper on recovery lays out the "Basic Tasks Of Recovery" as adopted from work by Curtis 1997 and Copeland 1997. These tasks are listed as follows;

- "Increasing self-understanding about one's identity; patterns of behaviour, environmental, attitudinal, behavioural, interpersonal or spiritual "triggers" successful coping strategies, as well as preferred professional interventions and supports."
- "Identifying the need for and arranging medical care and medications, when necessary"
- "Crisis planning, including a list of symptoms that indicate assistance needed in making decisions, a list of family members, supporters and professionals who are authorised to make decisions in a crisis. A list preferred, acceptable and unacceptable medications, treatment facilities and information about care of children, pets or other tasks that need to be taken care of during the crisis"
- "Building a support system, including friends, family, peers and others"
- "Developing ongoing coping, monitoring and responding strategies, such as distraction, "fighting back," seeking help, improving one's situation, self-soothing or escaping"
- "Developing advocacy skills and strategies to assure that one gets what one needs in the mental health system"
- "Developing a lifestyle that supports wellness, including valued roles, nutrition and exercise, sleep, light relaxation and private time, companionship and intimacy, pleasurable activities, pets, positive living space, meaningful activities and opportunities to contribute and spiritual practice"
- "Incorporating these knowledge and skills into a personal Wellness Recovery Action Plan"
- "Addressing any specific issues that are relevant to one's recovery"

The use of this type of list may be important in helping someone cope in the community but the expectation is still one of non-recovery. The prevailing theme is one in which the emphasis is upon preparing for the next crisis rather than getting on with your life. This importance placed on preparation for crisis can only be valid as part of a recovery agenda, if it is considered as part of a transitional programme towards recovery rather than the goal in its own right.

Central to the "basic tasks" model is the basic assumption that professional intervention is both essential and desirable. Within mental health services those who are defining social and clinical recovery are professionals who are themselves victims of their own belief systems about illness. This means that the definitions used for recovery will be rooted in a medical model rather than in a personal and subjective model.

This medicalisation even within social recovery is evident in the terminology used throughout the basic tasks in recovery framework listed above. Understanding the use of language is important if we are to understand the failure of the mental health system to achieve sustainable recovery on a large scale. The "basic tasks" framework is littered with the language of mental illness rather than the language of recovery. Throughout words and phrases such as coping strategies, professional interventions, supports, medical care, medication, symptoms, assistance, treatment facilities, crisis, distraction and ongoing coping monitoring and responding strategies are used as tools for the recovered rather than tools towards recovery.

I have chosen to describe the methodology used as one based on non-recovery because of the prominence placed on the notion of illness rather than wellness. Whilst it is true that many of the elements used by both Warner and Carling are important to the recovery process, it must be realised that their agendas have their foundations within the psychiatric system and therefore are based on the premise that illness is in essence biological in construct. This means that all interventions or techniques used by professionals will retain this biological causation as the focus of treatment and by implication the focus of recovery.

Conclusion

Given that this is the case then surely the only conclusion that can be reached is that within psychiatry social recovery is a myth, and is used by professionals as a way of monitoring and ensuring compliance, it is in fact nothing more than a means to a dead end. Both Warner and Carling reinforce this view, for Warner it is clear that it does not matter whether you measure clinical features such as psychosis or anxiety or social features such as number of friends or sexual functioning they both have an equal value in the measurement of recovery. The reality for the client is that social functioning is affected by the treatment they receive therefore there is a direct correlation between clinical and social recovery though it is not the one that psychiatrists would have us believe.

Construction, Deconstruction and Reconstruction

Power Or Empower Is That The Question?

I am one of those who hold to the idea that the process of personal recovery has at its very heart the reclamation of personal power. In order for the journey of recovery to be successful I believe that it is important to deconstruct the power of the psychiatric system and to reconstruct power as a personal commodity.

The present psychiatric system is rooted almost entirely in the perceived power of the psychiatric professional. I use the term perceived power rather than real power, for much of the power a psychiatric professional has does not come from them it is given to them by the State. This means that professional power is in essence politically based rather than knowledge or practice based. It also follows that the extent and level of their power is under the control of the politicians. The fact that the state has invested or entrusted this power into the keeping of the psychiatric profession at the present time does not mean that this will always be the case.

Many of us have spent and continue to spend much of our time trying to change the views of mental health professionals on the assumption that they have the power that creates, drives and maintains the present system. This assumption is an assumption too far; though there is no doubt that the professional both administers the mental health system and as a result makes choices for those who are patients within the system I do doubt whether they have as much power as we seem to give them. The power given to them by the state or their legal power, though too much, is never the less limited to the letter if not the spirit of the law. The bulk of their power comes not from the State but from the power ceded to them by carers, family and service users.

Within any type of health system this ceding of power is a normal process. Ask yourself what happens when you go to your General Practitioner? I may go to see him or her with a problem with our hearing. I start by telling him or her what the problem is e.g. "I am having trouble hearing in my left ear." With these words I do two things, firstly I expect him or her to find out what is wrong and resolve it. Secondly I put myself in his or her hands in other words I

give up personal autonomy (power). The doctor may decide to refer me on to a specialist
And when I see the specialist I will once again hand over my personal autonomy to a doctor. The expectation is however that once the doctor has made his or her diagnoses and spoke to me about the available treatment options he or she will allow me to reclaim my personal autonomy (power).

Like me most people do not see a psychiatrist or a psychiatric professional until their teenage years or later and by then our complaint response to the medical profession is well established. Our expectation of the psychiatric professional will be similar to the expectation we have of any other health professional, in that we will view our handing over of our personal autonomy as a transitory thing. The reality for many is however most certainly different in that psychiatry through its practice makes it almost impossible for us to reclaim our personal power.

The first hurdle we face in the recovery process then is finding a way to take back power. There is an ongoing attempt to address this power issue within mental health. This has resulted in the creation of the notion of "empowerment". Empowerment in general and empowering users in particular has become the politically correctness of the mental health system. Unfortunately this political correctness has not led to a change in practice only a change in language and in effect has failed to deliver autonomy to the service user. One of the reasons for the failure of this "empowering approach" is rooted in our failure to understand one of the fundamental truths about power; That is, that power is taken not given. If we look at the history of many of the campaigns for freedom or equality we can see that it was the perceived threat too the establishment (those who wield power) that made the establishment cede power.

Women in the United Kingdom are a case in point, they won the vote they were not merely given the vote. The role of the suffragettes in this fight for emancipation cannot, when looking at history be denied (though the establishment try to do so). Women were jailed, forcibly fed and died in the battle to win the vote. It was their sacrifice that forced the State to concede the vote. Gay people had to fight to win the right to live a particular lifestyle, they demanded and took the right to live their lives as they saw fit. They did this by "coming out of the closet" and demanding acceptance. This was against the coming out that forced the law to be changed. The twentieth century also saw a great deal of colonies claiming independence from their colonial masters. Many of these colonies had to fight bloody wars to achieve their independence. It was not so much that these colonies were given freedom much more it was the case that they took their freedom and the colonisers merely gave way to the inevitable.

I have applied the same principles to the issues of power faced by those who use mental health services and have come to the conclusion that the reclamation of power is something that is essential in any recovery process. Taking or reclaiming power does conflict with the empower approach that has been adopted by the system. The conflicts that exist between these two approaches to power do not in itself mean that the two approaches cannot work together. I prefer to call the conflicts that exist between the two, contradictions. This viewpoint (contradictions rather than conflicts) allows us to analyse the issue of power using dialectical methodology, which in turn will allow us to explore these contradictions in a positive way.

The ideas surrounding the need to empower users are based on an admission by professionals that power is an issue. The real problem is not in their understanding that power is an issue but in the fact that they focus the issue of power as one that has the service user at its core. It is here that their analysis is flawed, for it is not the professionals' role to give power to clients. Their role should be to give up the power and hold over service users they have and by doing so create the conditions in which service users can reclaim power for themselves. Likewise it is not the role of the service user to passively wait to be empowered but to be active in taking back their personal power. This is not and will never be an easy thing for professionals or service users to do.

The problem that users and professionals face when dealing with the issues of giving up power should not be underestimated. Due to the way mental health systems are organised professionals are forced to work within a system that is based on defensive practice. Defensive practice by its very nature does not encourage any form of risk taking indeed it does the opposite and ensures that practice is conservative at best and oppressive at its worst. The no risk strategy creates the no recovery culture and leads to the very power struggle that all sides claim they wish to end.

Take no risks has become the new mantra of mental health services, and as long as this is the case recovery will not be a realistic option for the many. The minister of state responsible for mental health in the United Kingdom led the chant of the new mantra when at the National Mind conference in 1998 he stated that non-compliance was not an option within mental health. I believe that this statement denies many one of the fundamental requirements for recovery that is the fundamental right of a citizen to make choices. The right to choose treatment or to refuse treatment must be the service users. In the next two chapters I will explore choice further within the context of a recovery programme.

Recovering Recovery.

In the introduction I gave a personal account of the recovery process I went through. The introduction was based on a speech I gave in Maastricht in January 1999. After the speech I was in a bar talking to some of the delegates, one of them who is a friend of mine commented on the fact that he had enjoyed the first part of the speech, which was about people. He then went on to say that he had found the second part about self somewhat of a contradiction given my political beliefs. In this chapter I intend to develop further the issues I raised in the introduction by looking closely at my stepping-stones to recovery, focusing on the issues of self and ownership.

If recovery is not to be viewed as a clinical construct then we must develop a different context in which the notion of recovery can be discussed. Within the introduction I have contextualised recovery as personal with the individual being best placed to define what recovery is. This does not mean that recovery occurs in a vacuum and that the individual goes it alone separated from society. Rather I believe that recovery is a liberating experience, which is experienced through the politicisation of the self within the wider society. What we cannot get away from is the role that the self plays within the decision making process.

Descartes defines the notion of self within his famous phrase "I think therefore I am" I would contend however that self becomes clearer within the bastardisation of the phrase to "I think therefore I am, I think". The addition of the words I think at the end of the phrase completes the contradiction of Descartes words in understanding the role of self within society. The role of the self within recovery is much more difficult to define without appearing to fall into the trap of the heroic self.

It was this issue of the heroic self that created the problems for my friend. He felt that by emphasising the part played by self in the recovery process then the danger existed that self would be glorified, at the expense of the role that other people play within the individuals' recovery process. Throughout my career as a speaker many professionals have approached me to tell me how brave I have been in facing my madness. Is this then the heroic self that my friend is talking about for if it is, then the heroic self is a creation of others not self. If this is the case then the heroic self is not the real problem, the real problem is that of professional perception.

The four selfs that I discuss in the introduction, self-confidence, self-esteem, self-awareness and self-acceptance should not be interpreted as some have done as a route to recovery that is wholly done by the individual. Rather the four selfs can only be understood fully when they are seen in relationship to the individual's interactions with others. When we examine the four selfs in detail one realises that the contradiction that exists in the notion of self is that self cannot exist without others to validate its existence therefore one can argue that the emotional or psychological; self cannot, indeed does not, exist in a vacuum.

How can we understand self-esteem if we do not view self-esteem as an emotional and psychological response that we can recognise in both others and ourselves and further it is a response that is in constant change?

How can we understand the notion of being self-confident if there were not periods in our lives when we lacked confidence and were helped to gain that confidence by others? Remember the very first time we try something new such as driving a car, we need to learn from the beginning normally we would have someone teaching us until we were confident enough to do the thing for ourselves. How do we develop self-awareness if it is not through interactions within human awareness? The idea that we can go and discover ourselves through being totally alone all of the time is a myth. We may only be aware of how much we love someone when we lose them, but we had to have loved them in the first place to be fully aware of the pain that love can bring when it has ended. Accepting ourselves for what we are requires the same type of analysis of self, that is, understanding that other people are a prerequisite within any analysis of the self.

If self cannot exist in isolation and our understanding of self can only be defined in terms of the relationship between the individual and others. This would mean that self is in actual fact a series of complex relationships with others and that self can only be measured by the impact we have on others in terms of emotions and the effect that the others have on the individual's emotions in return. Though at first glance this may seem an unimportant point in terms of a recovery process, a closer look will hopefully show that the understanding of this notion of self is essential in understanding the process of recovery.

I believe that much of what we call mental illness is based on a collapse of the self through the destruction of those relationships, which validate the self. This destruction will often result in an individual being alienated from their society in which relationships are formed. Within my own life this can be seen in my relationship with things spiritual, the abuse I received at the hands of a priest has clearly affected not only my view of priests but also my view of all things spiritual. This has meant that I refuse at all levels of my life to acknowledge the possible existence of my own self-spirituality. This is not a matter of whether I believe in a spiritual dimension or not but a matter of protecting myself through refusing even to explore the possibility of the spiritual self. The need to protect myself is born out of my life experience at the hands of a spiritual leader. At the point in time that the abuse started my relationship with spirituality was severed.

If this were the fourteenth century my lack of spirituality would be deemed to be evil or a sign of possession or an illness of the mind and I might well end up incarcerated or even executed. Without doubt my ability to live and function in this period of history would be greatly affected by my inability to function at a spiritual level. Putting it another way, when I was young and wanted to become a priest my self was validated through my relationship with God via the Catholic Church when that relationship was destroyed I did not suddenly stop believing in God it was much more that I felt alienated from God. My life at this point had lost its main validation and as a consequence my life was in turmoil.

The questions that we need to address at this time are to my mind fairly simple and revolve around whether the experience of self is altered by life events. If this is the case are we dealing with mental illness or a crisis of the self as it relates to society?
The destruction of relationships can also be seen in other traumatic life events for example; whilst I was in hospital I met quite a few students that had their first psychotic breakdown during their first year at university. Most had left home for the first time and were living in halls of residence. They had left their family and friends and found it difficult to adjust to their new surroundings, (bear in mind that moving home is considered the second most stressful life event after a death within the family).

It is within this context that many of these students started to hear voices or see things or begin to believe things that others find hard to understand. The system saw these events as the onset of mental illness, and treated the patients accordingly. I believe it would have been more appropriate to view the breakdown as one of a dilution of the persons' identity caused by the breakdown of the persons' relationships due to the move from their hometowns. Speaking with these students it is clear that for most of them the psychosis far from being a result of their biology, was a response to loneliness and the alienation they felt. Most of those I spoke with said that they felt they had lost their identity as a member of a family that had led them to withdrawing from the college scene and into themselves. It was when they had withdrawn from the college society that voices and other experiences occurred, much the same as with lone yachtsmen who start to experience voices within their isolation.

Whilst it is difficult to argue that these students have suffered a destruction of self-identity there can be no doubt that the isolation they went through has caused a dilution of self. This is reflected in their lack of self-confidence, self-esteem, self-awareness and self-acceptance all traits of this group of patients. Indeed researchers such as Bentall and Haddock, Romme and Escher, Birchwood, Turkington and Chadwick have all commented on the role that self-esteem plays in the outcome for patients. Others such as Beck-Sander have looked at self-acceptance whilst Smith 1999 notes the importance of self-confidence and self-awareness in the recovery process. The process of the dilution of the self is not however caused by internal factors rather it is due to the external factors. In these cases it is leaving home, and the feeling of seclusion that this causes, that results in the individuals experiencing this level of mental distress. Therefore as before the self cannot be understood without an insight into the persons relationships prior to leaving home and in these cases the lack of relationships on the college campus.

The other factors that struck me about this group were that their traumas had essentially internal consequences. The majority of them heard their voices internally rather than through their ears, most of them had intrusive thoughts about themselves and the majority had considered suicide as an option. Though one can argue that most traumas result in mainly internal consequences, how the voices were experienced in the head is in my opinion significant. I believe that when voices are experienced in this way it is often a sign that the persons' identity is in crisis. That is, there is a danger that the identity of the person is to the person being destroyed by the inability of the individual to hold onto their self. It seems clear then that in working with people who are going through this experience we need to work in a way that re-establishes the self.

The voices that I experienced were external, that is, I heard them through my ears. I have already explored the voice of the priest, now I will explore the voice of my first partner Annabelle. Annabelle was my first lover and the first woman I made any type of commitment too. When she died her death had a profound effect on me, in that it determined much of my life from then on in. I did not hear her voice until many years after the event due to the fact that I had suppressed both Annabelle's death and my abuse at the hands of the priest. This meant that I refused on a conscious level to have any internal dialogue with myself about these events. The result of this refusal was that I never dealt with any of the feelings that these types of trauma engender and therefore I did everything I could to avoid these areas of my life.

As well as turning away from any spiritual dimension in my life I also turned my back on relationships that involved any degree of commitment on my part. Though I did these things without realising that I was doing them it appears obvious now that the reason for doing so was to protect myself from further hurt. In other words I was struggling to protect identity and to hold on to self. This means then, that denial for that is what I was doing has a primary protective function and far from being a negative way of dealing with trauma it can in the short to medium term be a positive way of protecting a fragile ego.

Suppressing ones' feelings is a normal coping strategy that many people employ in order to protect themselves from life events. I suppressed my feelings for many years before I was forced to face them. I now believe that the reason I heard voices was my refusal to explore and deal with those life events I had experienced. Though I was not prepared to even look at what had happened to my life on a conscious level, this did not mean that on an unconscious level my mind was doing the same. Indeed much of my thinking around my voices is based on my belief that the reason my voices appeared was to alert me to the fact that my life was not whole.

What I mean by this is that when we go through a major trauma, and refuse to deal with it we cannot successfully suppress our emotions forever, there comes a point where it must be dealt with. Continual refusal to even acknowledge the existence of a problem brings with the need to adopt ever more extreme coping mechanisms such as self-isolation or as in my case playing sport in a violent manner that went beyond the norm in the game. The fact that my voices started after an injury which stopped me playing rugby (my violent coping strategy) is indicative of the short-term usefulness of distraction type coping strategies.

Stripped of my means of dealing with my past gave the inner me the opportunity to relive my past experiences. Because of my continual refusal to acknowledge the past my inner self was left with no option but to externalise my experiences through the introduction of voices. I believe that it was my refusal to use the opportunity presented to me to explore the voices when they first started that caused me to be hospitalised. My refusal like many others is based on our societal belief that voices equate with insanity. This was the belief that I held myself at this time. The reality for me at this point in time was a simple one I was mad, somehow my secure self was gone to be replaced by a helpless and frightened self which felt controlled by the external voices I heard.
Like many others it took me some time before I sought professional help, like many others the response of the professionals was typical, in that they saw my problem as a biological one and offered me medication. Like many others I rejected their opinion of my experience and like many others I was forced into a conflict relationship instead of a recovery relationship with the psychiatric profession. Throughout this period of battle with psychiatry a perverse emphasis was placed on the role of the self. This was that it was taken for granted that my desire to be myself in the decision making process about myself was in actual fact nothing more than lack of insight on my part.

The frightened self was very much to the fore at this point, soon gave way to the angry frightened self that the psychiatric system perceived as aggression and part of the deterioration of my illness. This led to the continuation of the conflict that in turn led to the absence of a recovery. The focus of professionals in understanding feelings as part of the illness process also means that they perceive "my self" as damaged and in need of repair.

It is no wonder then that in this system many of us feel that our very identities have been destroyed. It surely follows that the denial of self as expressed through the individuals' experience or behaviour by service providers will lead to the individual eventually denying their experience in order to keep the peace. This compliance in turn allows the professional to claim a moral and scientific authority over both the individual and society as a whole.

Earlier in the book we looked at how this moral and scientific authority is based on poorly researched ideas around defining clinical and social recovery within the realms of mental ill health. This has meant that much of what we today call evidence based practice is rooted in assumptions about causation and effectiveness of treatment rather than the reality of the experience as understood by the client. I would argue that it is the failure by professionals to understand the reality of a person's experience that causes the individual's identity to be in danger of destruction not the progression of a biological illness. The real importance of the notion of self I am putting forward is that madness far from being an illness is for many a desperate attempt to preserve the self.

In concluding this analysis of the four selfs it must be stated that whilst I acknowledge that the self must be rooted and understood in societal terms in order that any construction would be valid. It is equally the case that the notion of self can become personal when the individual is alienated by the psychiatric system to such an extent that there is no collective with which the individual can engage. It would seem apparent then that essential to any recovery process is some form of collectivist approach.

Personally I found this approach within the Hearing Voices self help group; at the very first meeting I attended a member of the group asked me the question, "Do you hear voices" when I replied that I did she responded with " They are real you know". This validation of my experience as well as being a validation of my "self " was also a pivotal point in my recovery process. The self-help group of which I was a member became in a real sense my community; it became the place where I could explore the meaning of self through talking with others.

Indeed in a strange way the group almost became the self. I suppose the biggest change that occurred for me within the group was that I stopped being Ron Coleman the schizophrenic and became Ron Coleman the voice hearer. Although this was only the beginning of the recovery process it was a good beginning. I never cease to be amazed by the amount of people I meet who introduce themselves to me as their label they say things like "hello my name is John and I'm a schizophrenic". I guess there was a time when I did the same, however I would never introduce myself with "Hello I'm Ron Coleman and I'm a diabetic"(which I am) because being diabetic says nothing about my status in society.

Ownership.

Running hand in hand with self I have always placed great store in the idea of who has ownership within the experience of mental distress. This like self is a concept that can cause difficulty for some in that like self it appears on first sight to exclude all except the individual from the process. As with self, first impressions are deceptive, my belief is that taking ownership of our experience is in essence a political and liberating process and as such is essential to the recovery process. In this section of the book I will explore the reasons that I hold this particular belief about ownership.

In the introduction I argue that doctors or other professionals, carers, friends or lovers cannot own the client's experience only the individual can own their experience. I continue in the same vein, concluding that it is only through owning the experience can a person own the recovery. This statement is one I have made on many occasions without developing it further, yet it is probably the most important issue that I talk about. I hope that my need to develop this theme further is not considered by readers too much of a self-indulgence but rather as an opportunity to consider for yourselves the implications of who owns a person's experience and the importance of that ownership.

Within the realms of psychiatric practice it is accepted that the most powerful practitioner is the psychiatrist. Their power is rooted not only in the authority given to them by the state but also in their singular right to make diagnoses. It is this ownership of a supposed expert knowledge that gives them so much power over their clients. I would contend that the real expert of the client's experience is the client and it is they not the psychiatrists that own the knowledge that makes recovery a possibility.

The main problem that many people have with the construct of ownership is again around the connotations that are associated with the word ownership. For some the word ownership is seen as part and parcel of the Thatcherite cult of the individual and has no place in the development of system based on a collectivist or inclusion model. This would only be a valid argument if the ownership of a person's experience was already a collectivist matter and the individual was attempting to create an individualistic approach from something that was already held in common ownership. Since this common ownership is not in existence then the transitional phase must be the wresting of the ownership from the professionals for the client by the client.

In many ways there is a group of psychiatric patients who are the modern equivalent of the American black slaves, in that many find their whole lives owned by psychiatric professionals. Nonsense many will say but let us look at the comparisons. In the Politics of the Madhouse (Coleman 1998) I laid out the foundations of the client as a commodity that was bided for through a tendering process by agencies that were vying to provide the care services for the client.

In the Politics of the Madhouse I was concerned with the tendering process mainly as the method by which clients were alienated from both the system of care and the workers that provided the care. In this book I want to take this analysis further, my contention is that this tendering system can in some cases turn clients into properties that are bought and sold in an open auction. This may appear incredulous to the reader but it is my recent experience with the tendering system that has brought me to this conclusion.

Working in the system has meant that on the odd occasion I am involved in writing tenders it was during a tender in May 1999 that I first started making comparisons with the slave trade. The tender involved moving people out of a nursing home that offered twenty-four hour nursing care into the community with varying degrees of support to be offered to the clients. I confess that I did not think very much about the people involved as I was writing my part of the tender. It was only when I was at the presentation to the purchasers that I realised that there was a whole group of us talking about people as if they were property.

What I mean by this is that the group of clients we were talking about had no idea what was going on. They would never be consulted about which agency would take over the provision of their care. They were in effect being auctioned off with the main priority being cost. There is no way that this methodology of selling people can be justified as an ethical way of contracting services. The result of this particular tendering process was that the organisation that had been looking after the clients did not win the tendering process and the

clients were to be handed over to another organisation without even a
by your leave.

Only when the auction was over would the clients be informed that
their lives were now to be organised by a new master. I am not saying
that provider organisations involved in the tendering culture do not
care for their clients, they clearly do. I do think however, that many
provider organisations whilst *caring for* their clients do nothing that
proves that they really *care about* their clients. My view is that this
type of tendering process that does not involve the consumer of the
service in every aspect of the tender can have little or no health gain
for the consumer. Indeed I believe if anything it will in most cases be
detrimental to the recovery journey in that it devalues and
dehumanises the individual in much the same way that slavery did.

It is not only in the auction room can the similarity between slavery
and patient-hood be drawn. In the arena of some psychiatric practice
the similarity is all too clear. Take the example of accepting the
doctors diagnoses, failure to do so will mean that the client lacks
insight, which is of course, part of the client's illness.
If in refusing to accept the diagnoses the client refuses to accept the
treatment the client is then non-compliant, this of course is part of
the client's lack of insight and therefore part of their illness. The
doctor via the State can respond to this lack of insight by forcibly
treating the person. If the client decides to leave the hospital it is not
considered to be rational but once again part of their illness and once
again the doctor has the power to restrain or to have a client brought
back to the hospital by the police.

Compare the above with that of the black slave, once sold to a master
the slave is expected to accept their lot. Failure to do so is considered
as the slave being maladjusted. This non-acceptance is considered to
show a lack of understanding by the slave of their lot in life, that is, a
lack of insight. When the black slave complained or fought against
their treatment once again this was seen as non-compliance, a lack of
insight on the part of the slave. If the slave dared to escape, the slave
was considered to be acting irrationally, indeed was seen as ill and
would be brought back to their master forcibly.

There is a positive similarity between the slave and the psychiatric
problem patient and that is that though both groups could be bodily
imprisoned within their respective systems, neither system could
control the desire of the oppressed to be free. Indeed both groups

created their own freedom in the only place the system could never fully control them their minds.

Like the slave then freedom begins with the rejection of others right to own you in any way shape or form. Rejecting the ownership that others hold over your experience is to accept personally the ownership of the experience. It is also the first step in taking power back from the system. A major consequence of not reclaiming ownership from the system can be the breaking down and eventually the destruction of the individual's self-identity. When this destruction is complete the system has created yet another chronic patient. It was for this reason that I came to the conclusion that ownership despite the political connotations as an essential part of the recovery process.

In the next chapter it is my intention to take these two elements, self and ownership and by adding the two elements of choice and people create a simple programme of recovery.

Choice Ownership People & Self

The C.O.P.S. Recovery Programme

There is very little point in criticising our present system if there is no alternative to put forward. In this chapter I intend to argue that there is a viable alternative way in which people with mental health problems can recover. Like any other journey, the recovery journey has an itinerary. The itinerary I will be using is called the C.O.P.S. recovery programme. COPS stands for choice, ownership, people & self. The programme is based on the elements that I believe were responsible for my own recovery. COPS is not a programme of clinical or social recovery though there may be outcomes that equate with these models of recovery rather it is a programme for personal recovery.

Recovery is essentially a personal thing and as such is experienced differently by each individual. There are, however some stepping-stones that are consistent amongst people who successfully recover and it these that are the stepping stones that make up the COPS programme.

Choice.

Most people in our society regard choice as a fundamental right and rightly so, indeed one can argue that the level of sophistication of a society can be measured by the level of choice an individual can make within society. Within democracies politicians go to great lengths to foster the notion of choice as the bedrock of society. The commission on social justice in the UK in their report "Social Justice strategies for national renewal"(1994) gave as one of their four propositions on social justice the following;

"We must promote real choices across the life-cycle, in the balance of employment, family, education, leisure and retirement."

Promoting these choices for every citizen is essential if a society is to be regarded as just argues the commission. I would agree with this argument and would argue further that for society to deny citizens these choices would make a society unjust. When the state uses its power to deny psychiatric patients' choice then the state is acting unjustly by denying them a chance of recovery.

Choice is one of the central themes that is time and time again misconstrued by services to mean that they make the decisions. Even where there is an element of choice it is often only cosmetic in that rarely are the choices offered really meaningful. Two good examples of this are in the areas of treatment and accommodation. All too often the notion of choice is lost in these areas with clients being offered only the choice between one drug or other in terms of treatment, despite the fact that the patients charter clearly states that all alternatives should be discussed with the client. The problem here is one that both the client and the medical staff jointly share the responsibility for resolving. There is no doubt that many doctors have no idea what alternatives are available to them beyond medication and they and their professional bodies must take the responsibility for rectifying this situation. Clients and their advocates must also take the responsibility for challenging the medics by pointing out the rights that clients have under the charter and asking why alternative treatments have not been considered.

Choice in accommodation is the other area where frankly we never learn any of the lessons from past mistakes. In the inner cities it is still the normal practice to move vulnerable clients out of acute wards back into poor housing or into run down estates that only increases their vulnerability and expedites their return to the acute unit. In many mental health services there is little or no choice offered in accommodation that develops the recovery potential of the client.
Indeed one could surely argue that often when we discharge clients back to the environment from which they came we do nothing more than set them up for relapse.

Real choice is not only having the ability to pick from a number of predetermined options it is also about having the power to add that which you as a consumer want, to those options. The professional perception of the things that people need is one of the greatest barriers to choice, since much of their perception is coloured by their professionalism. In order to achieve real choice it is essential that we start without preconceptions as to the real desires of the client.

More important than professional perception is the voice of the client if choice is to become a reality then service users must begin to exercise their voices they must make clear to professionals exactly what they want. One of my own memories of seeing the consultant in the ward round was how I always went into the ward round with lots of questions and came out with no answers. The main reason I never got any answers was that I always forgot the questions in the heat of the meeting. This was resolved when I finally agreed with my advocate to write down my questions before I went into the ward round. Though most of my questions still went unanswered I at least had the satisfaction of knowing I had asked them.

Much of the supposed choice in services revolves around the workings of the care programme approach (CPA) or case management approach (CMA). These two assessment tools would if used properly not only identify what professionals think the client needs but also what the client's aspirations are. All too often CPA has become nothing more than a medication review controlled by the medic. For this reason I believe that there is a need to be more direct in planning the recovery journey.

Making good plans will enable clients to plot their own journeys to recovery and ensure that they stay on course during the journey. There are many ways of planning that can be used which are person centred, the one that I prefer is a personal development plan much like the ones that most professionals use in their own workplaces. The reason for my preference is that the focus of this type of plan is very much on development rather than on care. This does not mean that we reject the concept of care indeed in my opinion working in this way can only enhance the quality of care provided by adding the notion of 'caring about' to the existing 'caring for' framework. Like most planning the personal development plan requires the person to answer a series of questions, the following are a selection the types of questions that may be asked;

1) What areas of your life do you consider have gone particularly well over the last six months?
2) What can be done by yourself or others to build on your successes?
3) What areas of your life have not gone so well in the last six months?
4) Have there been any particular barriers, difficulties or problems that have caused these parts of your life not to go so well?
5) What can you do by yourself to resolve these problems?
6) What can others do to help you resolve these problems?

7) What do you want to achieve over the next six months?
8) Which of these goals can you achieve on your own?
9) Which of these goals do you require help to achieve?
10)   Who can help you achieve these goals?

All of the above questions may appear straight forward but when was the last time we were asked them by others or indeed asked ourselves any of them. These questions are fairly open-ended in that they can relate to health, social activities, employment or training. They also allow the client to look at the strengths, weaknesses, opportunities and threats in their personal life. This SWOT analysis can if used properly by all concerned lead the recovery process by allowing the client to monitor their own progress against the goals they have set themselves.

One of the most important aspects of choice is in choosing the people that support the client. The usual practice of appointing a key-worker to work with the client without consulting the client is not only wrong but can in some circumstances be dangerous both to the client and the professional. How often do we ask both the client and the key-worker whether they are happy working together? Even if we did ask them and found that they were unhappy, would we act on the answer? I would hope so, though I fear the system would not respond in an appropriate way. This danger has nothing to do with the threat of violence posed by the client but the mess that will occur if there is no positive relationship between the client and the professional.

In services that do allow the client to choose their own support workers both the clients and the workers agree that this system of appointing staff eliminates many of the relationship problems that the traditional system creates. The other identified benefit was that a trusting relationship was established much more quickly using this system thereby speeding the recovery process. Even if the system cannot adopt a method that allows the client to choose their paid supports it must at the very least find a way to allow the client to change their paid supports if they wish to do so. If this simple step could be achieved then it is my opinion that the benefit in terms of recovery will far outweigh any loss of face that may occur amongst professionals.

The Professional as an Agent of Recovery.

The focus of the book has up to this point concentrated on the role of the client in the recovery process. In this chapter I will explore the role of the professional both individually and as part of a team approach in the recovery process.

One of the big myths about the pre-neuroleptic psychiatric system is that people went into this system and never came out. This clearly was not the case; indeed of those clients diagnosed as having schizophrenia fully one third recovered and left the hospital. This was due in no small measure to the interventions carried out by nursing staff. Most of these interventions would in our present system be called psychosocial interventions and be seen as the preserve of the clinical psychologist. Since the introduction of major tranquillisers in the mid 1950s the professional role has changed from one of pro-action to one of reaction or in many cases inaction.

There has however always been a group of professionals who have sought to do things differently. Psychiatrists from the days of Jung through Laing and Saaz to those of today like Romme, Thomas, Bracken, Dean and Sashidurhan have striven tirelessly often against mainstream thinking to effect change in both attitudes and practice within the system. Within Psychiatric nursing, Brooker, Gourney, Butterworth, Barker, Eagan, Johnstone and Smith have all in differing ways pushed to the fore the recovery role of the nurse. Psychologists such as Tarrier, Birchwood, Chadwick, Bentall and Haddock have developed the use of cognitive forms of treatment for people with psychotic symptoms. Another group of psychologists has taken a political view of psychiatry; these include Parker Johnstone and Mclaughlin.

Though I do not agree with all of the above it must be stated that they were or are doing something different often in the face of opposition from other colleagues. Much of the present day opposition to the biomedical form of psychiatry has rooted itself in the theories developed by one or more of these professionals.

In psychosis the coping strategy enhancement work of Tarrier et al though now seen by many as only having short- term benefits was significant far beyond its benefits to the client group. The reason for this was that for the first time since Jung an effective way of working with clients who were actively psychotic using psychological methodology had been developed and tested. The most important aspect of Tarrier's work was that it opened the floodgates for others to follow. This was quickly done by others such as Bentall and Haddock via their focusing technique and by Birchwood et al through their early intervention programme.

Parker and the critical psychologists added a new dimension through their
De-constructive approach to mental illness which allowed a new political basis for mental health users to root their opposition to the system. In the introduction to "Deconstructing Psychopathology" the authors write;

"As we go through the book we show why it is necessary to "deconstruct" psychopathology, and describe what we mean by "practical deconstruction"......... As we unravel, deconstruct traditional notions in the following chapters, we suggest strategies for change, and hope that you will be inspired in building, reconstructing something better. (page viii)

It is within these strategies for change that I believe one can find hope for the implementation of a recovery driven psychiatric system. Though in reality there is nothing new in the strategies within the book its importance for me is in the academic weight of the writers and its politicisation of the psychiatric system. Mclauglins chapter on the development of the Hearing Voices Network focuses on the importance of self-help in the recovery process. This chapter is a must for professionals who wish to set up hearing voices groups. More than this it is a chapter of hope for those who are distressed by negative voices giving them as it does a new way of dealing with their experience.

One of the great myths of the hearing voices network is that all the groups have been set up and run by voice hearers, running alongside this myth and equally wrong is the view that all hearing voices groups have been set up and run by professionals. The truth as usual lies somewhere in the middle of these two myths, groups have been set up and run by both professionals and voice hearers. It is not my role to make any judgement about which method of setting up groups is best, rather in this chapter I will explore how professionals can enable groups such as voices groups to develop in such a way that facilitates recovery.

Many professionals that I have talked to who have set up hearing voices groups have told me that one of the main things that has struck them on a personal level has been the amount of time it takes. They started groups thinking that it would meet once a week for an hour or two and that after each meeting it would be over until the next week. They soon discovered that nothing could be further from the truth and far from the group taking up an hour or two of their time each week, the group would very quickly consume a day or two of their time every week.

I believe that this process is nothing more than natural, in that what often happens in these type of self help groups is that the group bonds very quickly and becomes more than just a place where people talk about their voices or self-harm or beliefs. For many clients the group is a place where lives are shared, a place where their pain and distress is disclosed to an extent that there have been groups in which I have sat where the pain and distress has been almost tangible, almost solid and very real.

In these situations, the idea that the professional can fully remain an objective observer, is a nonsensical notion, professionals are after all human. There is no doubt that professionals involved in hearing voices groups find themselves changing as the group develops. One of them told me they felt as though the group had become part of their personal recovery. This was not a recovery from illness but the recovery of their personal identity over their professional identity. He told me that for the first time in a long time he felt he was doing what he had been trained to do. When I asked him to clarify this further he responded by telling me that when he had come into the nursing profession he had thought that his work would involve healing people, until the voices group his reality had been somewhat different. He went on to tell me that the real buzz for him was that as a practitioner he was now proactive in the recovery process.

The other important thing for him was that he believed that through the self-help group, voice hearers had begun to take control over their own lives. For him this meant that those voice hearers in the group who were also in his case-load had started on what he calls the discharge road, indeed within a year of the group starting he saw clients within the group being discharged from the system. He is now committed to staying in his profession and not leaving as he planned to do prior to his involvement in setting up the self-help group.

McLauglin in his analysis of the hearing voices network states:

" The Hearing Voices Network (HVN) challenges the 'reality' of mental illness, and redefines areas of experience outside the psychiatric apparatus"

This redefinition of experience also happens to professionals when like the person above they start to think about recovery and 'wellness' instead of illness. Thinking in terms of wellness shifts the professional focus towards person centred approaches. These go far beyond our current care programme and case management approaches to care and professionals find for themselves, a redefinition "of experience outside the psychiatric apparatus".

This is perhaps best seen in how nurses changed their practice when they started to work in the community instead of the hospital. By basing themselves in the community nurses came face to face with the reality of their clients lives. They saw the poverty, stigma and loneliness that their clients endured on a daily basis. In many instances nurses found themselves acting as advocates for their clients dealing with benefit agencies, housing departments and such like. This changing role caused many to question not only the values of society but also the treatment regimes that they were responsible for.

Whilst this move to the community and the changing role are important in developing the recovery role of nursing the most important development was the extent to which nurses started questioning the treatment regimes. I believe that this questioning is the first factor for any professional wanting to change how they work. The need to question is also an essential tool that professionals must use when working with clients. Not only should they question society and their clinical interventions they should also question things such as their clients beliefs and behaviours. Indeed I would go further and say that the role of the professional is to question everything. Questions are at the core of the recovery process for professionals and because of this it is important that when working with clients that the right questions are asked.

One of the main weaknesses professionals have is their reliance on previous notes about the client when they (the professional) receive the referral. In my opinion the mistake that many make at this point is to work from the referral letter or the accompanying notes rather than start with a blank sheet.

If the professional is going to work within a recovery framework it is essential that they start from scratch and that means assessing the client as if it was their first time in the system. The blind acceptance of referral data is tantamount to saying that nothing has or can change for the client. In North Birmingham the Assertive Outreach Team in the Sutton & Kingstanding locality have started to use a personal recovery plan with those clients who wish to use it. The team all agreed on the importance of moving towards a recovery model of working. This type of plan is not some rocket science type advance in the planning of care, rather it is a common-sense approach to people and their problems.

From the very beginning the plan puts the client at the centre of the process. The very first sentence states,

" This recovery plan is intended to help you to identify what you need to do to make your life how "*you*" would like it to be." (italics my emphasis)

The emphasise on 'you' runs throughout the plan, with clients having the freedom as to whether to use the plan or not. The client decides when to complete it, how long to take when filling it in, who should help them complete it, where the finished plan or copies of the plan will be kept and who can have access to the plan.

The plan also gives the following definition of recovery,

" 'Recovery' means different things to different people. It is not necessarily about the complete disappearance of mental distress and symptoms. For some of us, it means learning to cope with our difficulties, gaining control over our lives, achieving our goals, developing our skills and fulfilling our dreams. None of these things will happen overnight or without a considerable amount of effort from you."

Clients are told that they can leave bits of the plan out if they feel it does not apply to them. Another point the plan makes is that if people cannot be honest to themselves or take responsibility for themselves or be committed to their own recovery, then they are probably not ready to use the plan. This is the type of honest planning that is needed by all sides if a recovery model is to work.

The most important point of all is the fact that both the professionals in the team and the clients that use the services have developed the plan. This has meant that the honesty we mentioned earlier has been on both sides. The authors emphasise this point stating,

"We realised that often professional 'assessments' concentrate too much upon difficulties, diagnosis and symptoms, but neglect strengths, priorities and positives. Some of us (the professionals) believe that it would be more beneficial to concentrate more upon strengths, as these could be developed to overcome some of the difficulties."

It is this type of honesty that can break down the barriers that have existed between professionals and clients. With the breaking of these barriers comes new terms of engagement between professionals and clients that can turn assertive outreach from being perceived as aggressive into an active outreach based on positive engagement. Using this type of recovery plan especially its use by an assertive outreach team goes a long way to making positive engagement a reality.

The content of the plan is again simple to understand and is divided into seven sections these are,

1) Stage One: What recovery means to me.
2) Stage Two: About myself
3) Stage Three: Difficulties
4) Stage Four: Coping
5) Stage Five: The mental health system and treatments
6) Stage Six: Plans for change
7) Stage Seven: Your personal development plan

It is worth noting at this point that it is not until stage seven (the final stage) that the client starts their personal development planning. The reason for this is that the first six stages of the plan are essentially information gathering and it is by looking back through the other six stages that will enable the client to create an effective development plan. A copy of the plan can be found in the appendix of this book.

For any recovery plan to be workable it requires a joint approach indeed an alliance between the professional and client involved. This planning tool without doubt does exactly that in that it cannot work without the active participation of both sides. The role of the professional within the recovery process becomes ever clearer it is that of an enabler. It is their work as an enabler that allows professionals to reach their full potential as agents of recovery.

How many times have you heard professionals say that the biggest problem they have is the size of their caseloads and because of this they lack the time to deliver the quality of service they feel their clients deserve? Like many others I believe that the answer to this problem must be a sizeable reduction in the caseloads carried by professionals. I would argue that for a professional to be fully effective a case-load should be restricted to eight, this would mean that each client would have a half day and the professional would have a whole day for meetings and paperwork. Unfortunately such a shift in method is unlikely to happen in the present climate, we therefore need to find other ways of creating quality time for clients.

"Making Recovery a Reality" a recovery programme developed by Coleman & Smith is one attempt to resolve this problem. The programme uses developmental method to engage clients and professionals on a recovery journey. Again the programme is simple to use and has its roots in the notion that recovery is a developmental process and that all clients are on the recovery continuum and that professionals can facilitate the clients move along the continuum towards discharge (recovery).

The aim of the programme is to work with the team in developing the practice skills necessary to facilitate recovery. The programme requires the team to start a full reassessment of all clients. This review is then used to place the client into one of three following groups:

1) Group one is those clients who have both the potential and the desire or motivation to recover.
2) Group two is those clients who have the potential but lack the confidence, desire or motivation to recover.
3) Group three is those clients who for various reasons have essentially been viewed as having no hope by the system.

Once the clients have been assigned a group the next task is to complete a personal development plan with each client. This plan would follow the same format as the Kingstanding recovery plan. The personal development plan would also look closely at areas of the client's experience, which have yet to be resolved. For example if during the review it was found that a client was hearing persistent negative voices then part of the development plan might be to work with the person's voices to enable them to cope better with the experience. In this scenario the team would employ various tools, such as the Maastricht Interview Schedule, the Working with Voices workbook, Cognitive Behavioural Therapy, and a Hearing Voices Self-help Group. The same types of interventions would be applied to problems such as self-harm, alternative beliefs, visions and other experiences.

On the face of it, it looks like what all this would do is to increase the workload on the team. It most certainly would if members of the team thought they had to do all of these things themselves. If however we look at how this could be implemented then a different picture can be painted. The idea behind distributing the clients into the three groups is twofold.

1) To fast-track as many clients out of the system as quickly as possible. Though this may appear to favour the clients in group one, in the medium term it will in actual fact benefit all clients since much of the work with group one can be done as a group. This will save time in that clients will be 'seen' by the professional regularly and if there is a need for a one to one meeting it can be arranged at this time.
2) To enable the remaining clients to enter the fast-track process through facilitating the implementation of their personal recovery plans. Once again much of this work can be done in groups, indeed the aim is to encourage this group to be in the same group meetings as those in the fast track. This method is commonly called peer support in papers I prefer the term self-help.

The programme not only develops the clients' recovery potential it has been designed to develop the teams' practice skills through ongoing training these training needs are identified via the recovery plans of the client group. As each client completes their recovery plan the team identify which of the skills they lack that are required to work with the client. When the needs of the team have been identified then members of the team will be given the appropriate training to meet these needs. The other area that the teams are encouraged to develop is their team meetings, instead of using them to discuss all of the clients briefly, they are encouraged to focus on only one or two clients who may be having a difficult time. The rational behind this is simple focusing on one or two clients allows the team time to explore different possibilities for these clients in much greater depth than would normally be possible in a team meeting. I am always amazed at the ideas that are generated by teams when they try this approach.

As you can see all we have done in this programme is to bring together a number of already existing practices and gave them equal validity within one team. This has also meant that the division between different professions in the team has been diluted. A team operating in this way will have all of the elements of any good multi-disciplinary team. In one of the teams I work with we have nursing staff, psychology staff, occupational therapists, support workers, peer workers and medics all working as equals, doing what is needed when it is needed. When all of these elements are working together using the same plan with the individual then recovery becomes a reality.

One other area of professional involvement is in self-help groups though I touched on it earlier in the chapter I intend now to look at one professional's experience of being a facilitator of a group. There are many debates about the role of professionals in the self-help movement, mainly about whether they should be involved at any level within self-help groups. It is not my intention in this book to involve myself in the pros and cons of this debate. I will instead adopt the position that we took in the Hearing Voices Network that professionals within the group were allies and were there because they believed that the group had real value for voice hearer

Since 1992 I have had the good fortune to be involved in the setting up of hearing voices groups both in the UK and abroad, in many cases I have been invited to come to an area by professionals who were keen to see self-help groups established. Often the professionals involved wanted to help set up a group and then withdraw and leave the voice hearers to get on with it. In my experience this withdrawal process has taken much longer than they originally thought, not due to the professionals wanting to hold onto the group, but to the fact that voice hearers wanted the professionals to remain as part of the group.

I visited one such group in England in 1998 and again almost exactly one year later. The membership of the group including the professional had remained almost the same since my first visit, what had changed since the first visit was the people in the group. The group was essentially made up of people who were considered to be chronic patients, many professionals had written them off as hopeless cases and their futures were defined in terms of long-term care.

What a difference a year can make, whereas on my first visit the members of the group said little and in many cases nothing, now they were all talking. They were not just talking about general things they were talking about their voices and other experiences that had led them into the psychiatric system. They were also talking about how they coped with their experiences, encouraging each other to try different strategies' members had found helpful. The one thing that was central to the group's success they all agreed was the consistency not only of the voice hearers attending but the fact that the same professional had been part of the group since the beginning.

As far as the group was concerned the professional held an enabling function within the group in that he was able to answer many of the clinical questions that members of the group might have. He had an educational role within the group in that he would provide information on subjects such as diagnoses, side effects of medication and other treatments that were available. The professional involved told me that the group was both challenging and rewarding and that the group had changed many of the members perspectives on what was happening to them. It had also changed his perspective of his role within the care of an individual changing the focus from caring for a person to caring about the person. Though none of the group are yet ready for discharge there can be no doubt that they have moved a long way on the recovery continuum. The role of the professional within these types of self help groups is pivotal in the recovery of many and within this situation the professional can indeed be described as an agent of recovery.

Till now I have concentrated on working within a group environment and said little about one to one work, the remainder of this chapter will focus on working with individuals. Even when we work in a person centred way there is a danger that what we will end up doing is turning person centred working into a model. The minute we do this we will have failed for the very act of creating the model denies the individualistic approach, not that this will matter for we are conditioned via training to think in terms of models. To counter this I will now introduce you to my preferred model for working with individuals.

This model is called the PIE Model. PIE is in my opinion the most advanced model of care in that if used properly it makes no assumptions either overtly or covertly. PIE stands for play it by ear and it is the only way that you can truly take a person centred approach and applies it on numerous people. Using the PIE model it allows you to easily create a service around a person rather than fitting a person into the existing services. Since in essence it is reactive in that you are developing the service in response to the present circumstances and since most services even in acute care are based on this principal of response then this model should prove no problem for professionals to implement.

I first used play it by ear in the mid 1990s' when I was approached by a woman
(I will call her Jenny; she has given me permission to write her story)
Who asked me if I would work with her to resolve her voices; at that time I did not work with individuals so I told her no. Jenny was one of these people who did not take no for an answer and she took to asking me at regular intervals if I would reconsider and work with her, eventually she wore me down and I agreed to meet with her to discuss the possibilities of working together. The first time we met we spent three or four hours discussing her life history and the voices that she heard. I confess that my agenda was to make this first meeting our last but after our first meeting I was hooked and we agreed to meet again to start working through her voices. The following is a précis of the work we did together and the results of our work or should I say her work.

Jenny

The first thing Jenny did was to tell her life story, which in a very shortened version went like this; when Jenny was a child she lived with her mum who was divorced from her father and she had no contact with her dad. Her mother met a new man who Jenny said was okay at first, her mother married the new man and Jenny got herself a step-dad. Although everything was good at the beginning, it was not long before her new step-dad took an interest in Jenny not as a daughter but as an object that he could abuse. Jenny was abused by her step-dad for about two years before she finally told her grandmother what was happening to her. The grandmother told Jenny's mother what was going on but her mother refused to believe it, finally in frustration grandmother took Jenny to live with her and brought Jenny up. Her grandmother did not go to the authorities for fear that she too would lose Jenny, Jenny was also very clear that she did not fault her grandmother for this, indeed Jenny felt her grandmother had done a good job in bringing her up. Jenny married when she was in her late teens and divorced in her mid-twenties she had two children during her marriage. Her grandmother died when she was twenty-two and she felt very alone since she did not talk to her mother who was still married to Jenny's abuser.

Jenny had started hearing an occasional voice when she was in her late teens but thought nothing of it. During the break-up of her marriage her voices had got much worse and she started hearing very negative voices, it was at this time that she came to the attention of the psychiatric services. She was eventually given a diagnosis of paranoid schizophrenia and put on various neuroleptics none of which relieved the voices. She was prone to self-harming and spent a lot of her hospital admissions being detained on sections of the mental health act. She had finally managed to bring her self-harm under control though she had not stopped completely, she had got this far through membership of a self-help group.

Jenny identified four voices, the first was male very negative, always abusive and commanding. This voice would tell her that it was her fault that she deserved everything that happened to her and that she was a slut. This voice she knew was the voice of her stepfather (her abuser). The second voice was in every way a contrast to the first voice it was female very positive, never abusive, it was advisory and everything it said was soothing and helpful. This voice would say that things would be okay that she (the voice) would protect Jenny. Jenny knew this to be the voice of her grandmother. The third voice was the voice of a female child who would do nothing but scream all the time. In one way this was the most difficult voice for Jenny in that it never made any sense. It was only after some time that Jenny identified the voice as the voice of herself when she was being abused. The final voice was a male voice that was a mixture of everything, it was both positive and negative, abusive and non-abusive, advisory and commanding indeed so much so we called it her neutral voice and she knew it to be the voice of her ex-husband. Once we had a life history and a voice profile Jenny then related her voices to her life history and decided that her real problem was not the voices but the fact that she had been sexually abused and that his issue had never been properly resolved.

Before we could go any further with the voices work Jenny had to carry out one of the most difficult and lonely tasks that anyone who has been abused has to do, that is she had to find herself innocent of any fault within the abuse. This is something that everyone who has been abused has to come to terms with at some point if recovery is going to become a reality. The voice of the abuser told Jenny that it was her fault that the abuse happened and like many people who hear the voice of their abuser or abusers Jenny was inclined to believe that she did play some part in leading him on.

It did not matter that I like many others told Jenny that she was the victim in this situation what mattered is what Jenny thought was the facts. Jenny had to put herself on trial and in order to do this she had to go through the experience again and again from every conceivable angle until she could say with real conviction I am innocent. This is no easy task and anyone who has done it will tell you that not only is it painful it is also exhausting and often initially it makes the voices worse. Once this was done Jenny and I discussed how best to work with the voices, her desire was to get rid of the voices though she knew that at best she would probably only succeed in developing coping strategies that would allow her to get on with her life.

We decided that the best way forward was to enter into dialogue with her voices and that we would do this with one voice at a time starting with the most positive voice first. In other words we would do what most professionals believe we should never do, that is actively engage with the voices. The first attempt was almost a complete disaster, with hindsight it was my fault as I underestimated the resistance that I would encounter from the voice of the grandmother. I started by asking Jenny if she would ask her grandmother if she would talk to me. Jenny's reply astonished me at the time, she (her grandmother) wanted to know why she should talk to me and why I wanted to help Jenny. It took three meetings before the grandmother would stop asking questions as to my motives and start talking about how we might help Jenny. *(After the whole process was over Jenny and I concluded that the questions her grandmother's voice was asking were in actual fact related to Jenny's own fears about the journey we were starting)* After the initial breakthrough grandmother agreed to help Jenny and I deal with the voice of the stepfather. We then decided that the next voice to approach was that of her ex-husband, this was a complete and utter waste of time the voice played games with us for weeks on end before we finally decided that there would be no help for Jenny from this voice. *(We came to the conclusion from this experience with the voice of the ex-husband that some voices have very little or no significance when you are working through the voice hearing experience, indeed that some voices are nothing more than red herrings)*

We then turned our attention to the child voice and to our horror found that not only would the child not engage in any way with me it would not engage in any way with Jenny either. We spent many hours trying to forge a relationship with the child to no avail. Eventually we turned to the grandmother for help and asked her to negotiate with Jenny the child, the grandmother agreed and she slowly managed to get Jenny the child to talk to us but initially only through her (the grandmother). Over time Jenny the child stopped screaming and did start to talk to us, she agreed that it was her that had to confront the abuser and we spent many hours preparing Jenny the child for this confrontation. *(We had in effect forgotten one of the rules of working with voices, which was to play to your strengths. We had started the process by enlisting the aid of the grandmother and then once getting it we had essentially left her out of the process. She was to be the key to Jenny the child as a voice as she had been the ally of Jenny when the abuse had occurred in if you like real time. It also made me acutely aware of the importance of the interactions between different voices that people hear)*

When the voice of Jenny the child told us she was ready to confront the abuser we decided to make two days available for the confrontation. Jenny arrived one Friday afternoon and we chatted for a couple of hours not about voices or how she was feeling but just relaxing. Then on the Saturday morning we got down to work. Jenny the child voice told the abuser exactly what she felt, she told him that it was him that should have left the family home, that it was he that was the perpetrator and her that was the victim. She old him that she was innocent and that he was guilty, that she had the right to hate him and no longer felt that she was evil. She repeated much of this over the course of the day, every time the abuser voice tried to regain control of the situation Jenny the child would be backed up by Jenny, the grandmother and myself. By the end of that day although we were exhausted we both knew something had changed and that much had now been resolved. Even now though it was not as we expected it to be, there were no great victory celebrations only the quiet that follows any major battle. It was some weeks later before we sat down together to look at what had happened since the day of the confrontation.

There had been some remarkable changes in the voices that Jenny was hearing; the abuser voice was no longer dominant though it was still there. We surmised from this that the reason it had not gone completely was that though Jenny had dealt with the abuse she could not become un-abused, that is she could not change what had happened only her response. The grandmother voice had now become dominant and that was okay for Jenny as it was as always a positive voice. It was the disappearance of the child voice that was the most significant change and we concluded that this had happened due to the end of the need for Jenny to disassociate from her past. Indeed we believe that Jenny the adult and Jenny the child voice became Jenny the person. These changes have now remained constant in her life for over four years, without doubt Jenny has reclaimed her life, she has recovered.

My role in this process was minimal I played only a bit part it was Jenny who did all the hard work I only created the space in which she could do this work. It is clear to me that this is one of the main roles that professionals can play when working with clients. Clients who are working through complex recovery journeys require this type of support to enable them to complete their journeys successfully. I cannot believe that this is an impossible shift for professionals to make indeed I would argue that many already do these types of interventions and that many more wish to. My only advice for professionals is simple do it.

Organisations as Vehicles of Recovery

If recovery is to become a reality for the many then organisations need to become vehicles of the recovery process this requires a change in the mindset of organisations and the development of a recovery platform that is value based.
Organisations being what they are must however believe it is in their best interests to make this move to recovery based services before they will do so.

Helen Glover in her discussion paper Uncovering Recovery Gives the following reasons as to why recovery based practice should be both adopted and developed she writes.

"Recovery issues do not solely pertain to the individual who experiences distress or illness but to the whole community including:
- Policy makers,
- Commissioners,
- Organisations that provide services,
- Practitioners,
- Those that use services,
- Those that play a significant role in the lives of people who experience mental illness / distress, and
- The general community at large.

While the interplay between these stakeholders appears hierarchical, it must be remembered that all players have a responsibility to look seriously at their role within recovery orientated service development and delivery.

This developing discussion is intended to facilitate understanding of recovery–orientated service delivery. It helps us to recognise how all stakeholders can interplay to provide what we understand as recovery practices. It also attempts to provide a value base for which recovery practice can be developed and delivered."

Reasons to adopt and develop recovery practice

- Services will be responsive to the needs of people with mental illness/distress

- Services, in being responsive, will be effective and efficient

- Services will have staff that feel valued and supported in their work

- Services will have staff that feel fulfilled in their work with people with mental illness / distress

- Service users will feel actively involved in their care

- Service users will inform and be fully informed on all issues pertaining to their recovery

- As planning is central to recovery practice, service users, significant others, and service providers will have prepared for contingencies and crises

- Recovery practice is forward and future focussed

- Service users, their significant others and service providers will develop collaborative partnerships in their work towards recovery.

- Coercion and control of people's actions will not dominate practice

- Evidence based knowledge and value based knowledge will co exist

- An articulated value base will underpin each service's/organisations practice

- Feedback will not be feared, but sought and embraced in the continual development of responsive and accessible services

- Partnerships between all key stakeholders, including community members and groups, will be active and visible

- People will move beyond the need for intensive service delivery

- Service users will be educated about recovery processes and the applicability to their lives

- The diversity of knowledge, experience and values of all stakeholders will be upheld

➤ Within a recovery framework, providing diagnosis and prognosis is secondary to developing meaning and understanding

➤ Inviting people to create a society where inclusion is a reality, and develop meaning to what is happening for them.

➤ A relationship based on equality where the mutuality of knowledge and experience is respected is more aligned with recovery relationships and outcomes."

Can we imagine our organizations making the changes required to implement a service system that adopts the above elements? For too many of us the answer will be no but does this mean we should just give up and go home? Again I would argue that the answer to this question is no. Rather than give up we should start looking at each of these 20 reasons given by Glover and seek to find ways in which they can be implemented in our own individual practice as well as within our organizations. Let us explore these reasons individually and look at what is already being done and also what could be done individually and organizationally to change the current ways of working.

1. Services will be responsive to the needs of people with mental illness/distress. In all of the organisations I have worked for or visited staff would say that they are responsive to peoples needs in times of mental turmoil. I would have to disagree with them and I believe that in far to many cases rather than being responsive to peoples needs we are in actual fact being reactive to peoples behaviours. As stated earlier in this book our current system is very good at reactive working being responsive though requires us to be proactive. Being responsive or proactive will not always mean keeping a person out of hospital but it might mean making the process of hospitalisation a different experience for the client. One example of how this can be achieved happened when I was working with a team in the West Midlands we were asked to visit a client who was known to the service and who was in a great deal of mental distress. The distress had reached the point that it was decided that he should come into hospital.

This had happened on numerous occasions in the past and the process had normally been, a mental health act assessment which would decide that he must come into hospital something which he was loath to do and would refuse to do which in turn meant a number of police would arrive and forcibly take him to the hospital where he would try to run away and end up being transferred to the locked ward. As a team we decided to try to do something different that would help break the cycle we were in with him. Three of us myself and two nurses went to visit him at home it was obvious to us that he was in a great deal of distress and flitting from personality to personality every few minutes (he had multiple personalities) we decided however that waiting for a mental health act assessment would not change anything for him so we agreed to try to negotiate with each of the personalities as they appeared with a view to a voluntary admission. One of his personalities decided he would like us to join him for a picnic so one of the nurses went to the local shop and bought some food for the picnic, which we had on the floor of his living room. We spent the next three hours with him negotiating his admission to hospital not only with the client but also with the consultant and the ward staff. For the first time in his life as a patient he agreed to come into the ward as a voluntary patient. When we arrived at the unit the consultant was waiting and we had a meeting with the client the ward team and our team where we discussed the plan for working with him. This was a clear example of responding to a crisis in a very different way. Although we had not prevented the crisis becoming an admission we had broken the pattern of admission and were able to work with the man in a much more proactive way.

2. Services, in being responsive, will be effective and efficient. As can be seen from the above story this was a much more effective and efficient way of working. I would argue that what we were able to do was create a therapeutic alliance with the client that was clearly different from the normal conflict based relationship we had with the client previously. This in turn had a knock on effect in that treatment was then subject to negotiation and discussion rather than compulsion. This of course meant that as a team we were working with the person rather than on the person clearly this is much more efficient and effective. The major benefit for our team in this situation

was that for many of us we felt as though we were doing our real jobs for the first time in some cases for many years.

3. Services will have staff that feel valued and supported in their work. One of the reasons we were able to work with this client was the position that senior management and the consultant had taken on the subject of recovery. The trust as an organisation had decided that they would adopt a recovery based approach to service delivery and the consultant involved believed in this approach so was prepared to take risks and support the team in taking these risks. She was not the type of consultant to immediately use medication or the mental health act in order to feel secure in her job, rather she believed in discussion and reaching agreement with all those involved and in doing this she effectively encouraged and supported staff, clients and carers. This in turn meant that staff felt that their views were heard and this meant that they felt valued as workers.

4. Services will have staff that feel fulfilled in their work with people with mental illness / distress. Once again the above story illustrates the fact that by working in a recovery based way staff as well as clients can derive great benefits. In the three years that I worked with this team I was aware of only two members of staff moving on and they went on to run new teams being set up within the trust. It is clear to me then, that where staff feel fulfilled in their roles as workers then staff retention rates will be higher with the added bonus of having not only a settled team but a client group that is much more secure and clear about the response they will receive from the service.

5. Service users will feel actively involved in their care. This seems such an obvious point that I almost left it out, yet my own experience of services should have made me realise that this is one of the areas in service delivery that we are still failing to get right. Often service user involvement in their care remains far from being an active process one which is either non existent or extremely passive. In order for this to change we need to move towards methods of planning that put the client at the centre of the process. The use of person centred planning methodology is not new in health care, it is an established approach within learning disabilities and it now needs to be implemented in mental health care. It is my

contention that failure to properly introduce person centred planning methods will not only stop users from being involved in their care but will make recovery as a goal almost impossible to achieve.

6. Service users will inform and be fully informed on all issues pertaining to their recovery. Mike Smith speaking at a conference in Birmingham in 1999 stated "Information and knowledge are power" personally I fully agree with this statement and believe that for too long services have used knowledge and information in a negative way. If services were to adopt the principle of being informed by their clients and in turn giving proper information to their clients then the difference to the quality of the relationship between service provider and service recipient would be positive for both sides. A good example of this would be around the issue of medication and the side effects of medication, if services told clients what the known side effects of their medication was then the rate of non compliance with meds would drop significantly. We know this because of the research carried out by John Donnague a pharmacist who found that clients who were fully aware of the side effects of the medication they were on were far less likely to stop taking their medication against medical advice. It makes sense therefore for services to buy into the notion of giving clients full information about all aspects of their care. This information must in turn be informed and developed through consultation with clients.

7. As planning is central to recovery practice, service users, significant others, and service providers will have prepared for contingencies and crises. It is essential that service providers and users prepare in advance for any crisis that may happen. Doing this recognises a number of important factors within a recovery platform these include the fact that recovery does not mean the absence of symptoms rather it is about getting on with your life and that a crisis may not need to end up in a hospital admission and a return to being a full time patient this can more often than not be avoided if good crisis resolution planning has been carried out. Though it is not possible to see into the future with our clients it is possible to ensure that as far as we can we develop strategies to deal with known triggers and historical responses to these triggers.

8. Recovery practice is forward and future focussed. If recovery is to become a reality in peoples lives then providers need to move

away from maintaining the status quo in which clients past histories determine the planning process towards one in which the desires, dreams and aspirations of our clients are at the centre of the process. Making this change would mean that hope would become a feature of service provision.

9. Service users, their significant others and service providers will develop collaborative partnerships in their work towards recovery. A service or organisation that is rooted in recovery would be active in developing collaborative working relationships with any and all stakeholders including the wider community. Developing these types of relationships will create the climate in which recovery is seen as the expected outcome for those with mental health problems. This in turn would clearly impact on how people with mental health problems are perceived by the wider community and help in the ongoing battle against stigma.

10. Coercion and control of people's actions will not dominate practice. In any service that is rooted in recovery it would be inconceivable that the service would see as one of its primary roles the use of force or even the threat of force as a means of ensuring compliance rather good recovery practice would have at its core negotiation and discussion seeking to find agreement through a collaborative approach rather than conflict through a macho approach to service provision. The use of any mental health legislation should become a last resort only used after all other approaches have been exhausted. Even in cases where the law is used the duration of coercion should be kept to a minimum. Seeking an agreed resolution must be a priority in cases where there is conflict between professionals and users failure to do this must surely hinder the recovery process.

11. Evidence based knowledge and value based knowledge will co exist. The current obsession with evidence based practice and the exclusion of almost any other way of thinking about service practice has in my opinion meant the dilution of the development of new skills within services. The biggest asset any professional will accrue as they develop their own practice is a knowledge base gained through experience, which will affect how they choose to practice. If alongside a good knowledge base we add a clear value base then it is clear that the impact for the client will be a positive one.

12. An articulated value base will underpin each service's/organisations practice. It is all very well to have a value base that is theoretically good but if the theory is not

translated to practice then it is worthless. For an organisation to adopt recovery practice makes it necessary for the organisation to adopt recovery values. Values such as believing in the clients' capacity to recover, accepting that clients are real experts in terms of their experience and taking considered risks are all essential to the recovery process. Without these types of values then recovery will simply be another buzzword that will pass into the annals of history.

13. Feedback will not be feared, but sought and embraced in the continual development of responsive and accessible services. Although most services claim to embrace user involvement in their services it has clearly been a major complaint from user groups that this is not the case. Services operating in a recovery based way will not fear feedback from clients, carers and others involved including their own staff rather they would view feedback as an opportunity to ensure that their services made changes as and when they were needed. Successful services would actively seek constructive criticism to enable them to remain both responsive and accessible to their clients.

14. Partnerships between all key stakeholders, including community members and groups, will be active and visible. All to often in our present system the concept of partnerships is one that is tokenistic. If services are to truly operate in partnership with all stakeholders then they must move towards having memorandums of understanding with stakeholders. This would put relationships between the main service provider and others on a formal footing and away from the informal often, toothless relationships that are currently in operation. This would without doubt create a tension between the provider and others but I for one believe that this would be a healthy tension.

15. People will move beyond the need for intensive service delivery. Services that operate on the basis of a recovery methodology would over a period of time move people out of the revolving door mentality by breaking the cycle through interventions designed to kick-start the recovery journey. Too many clients find themselves in services for life and too many services are designed in a way that allows this to happen. Recovery based services would have clear exit pathways for clients not into other mental health services but back to primary care services. The role then for mental health services would simply be to make themselves redundant in their clients' lives.

16. Service users will be educated about recovery processes and the applicability to their lives. Much has been made about psychosocial education for clients, in which we teach clients to recognise their triggers and how to detect the onset of symptoms. We even teach clients about their diagnoses so it would seem sensible to teach clients about the process of recovery and how to apply the process to their own lives.

17. The diversity of knowledge, experience and values of all stakeholders will be upheld. It is sad that in such a diverse society as the one in which we live that we need to address this issue at all. It is perhaps the worst indictment of our present mental health system that there is still a lack of respect for different point of views. This can best be seen in the continuing dominance of the medical model of mental illness, which despite the growing weight of evidence finds itself becoming ever more entrenched in its search for biological and genetic explanations for mental illness. A recovery approach would demand a shift away from the dominance of the medical model and the adoption of a holistic model of health care. The acceptance of an holistic approach to mental health would allow all stakeholders including the medical profession to participate in the recovery process as partners.

18. Within a recovery framework, providing diagnosis and prognosis is secondary to developing meaning and understanding. Romme and Escher in their seminal book accepting voices demonstrated this simple truth when their research indicated that some 70% of voice hearers could root their voice hearing experience in their lived experience. Their work is responsible for making many a recovery possible through their notion that psychosis is something that can be understood as a normal response to abnormal events. If services are to deliver the goods on recovery then much more time must be spent understanding the context of a persons experience and much less time on trying to make sense out of the medical professions understanding of the persons experience.

19. Inviting people to create a society where inclusion is a reality, and develop meaning to what is happening for them. Even if we convinced every service provider, every worker and every service user that recovery is the way forward it could end up counting for nothing if we fail to convince the wider community that recovery from mental health problems is not only to be desired but that it can be the reality of the many. This may

mean that we need to see ourselves as not only agents for recovery with our clients but also as agents for recovery within our wider society.

20. A relationship based on equality where the mutuality of knowledge and experience is both respected and is more aligned with recovery relationships and outcomes. Last but not least we come back to the relationship between worker and client. It is my opinion that this relationship is often a mirror image of the relationship between workers and management. If management do not have high expectations of their workforce then surely it follows that workers will not have high expectations of their clients. I am not saying that individual workers would not work differently rather that if there is a prevailing culture of maintenance within an organization then the culture itself will self perpetuate making the implementation of a recovery platform within the organization virtually impossible. Changing the culture to one of recovery demands that we accept as a given that all parties have an expertise that is essential to creating services that will deliver recovery outcomes.

Though getting organizations to work to a recovery outcome for clients may seem a daunting and difficult task never the less it is my belief that failure to move to this approach will not only impede recovery for clients but will indeed impede the recovery of psychiatry as health orientated service and keep it as an illness dominated institution. Moving away from a maintenance approach to mental health care is therefore a must for organizations if we are to provide services that are compatible with the desire of professionals, users, carers and the wider society to see effective and proactive mental health working towards recovery in our communities.

The road to recovery though difficult is I hope by now, no longer seen as impossible, there are some hard times ahead for clients and professionals both in their individual circumstances and from wider societal perspectives and in this final chapter I hope to deal with some of these issues.

Whilst reading through some of the drafts of this book Karen my partner commented on the fact that though I was dealing with recovery I had not written in any great detail about the bane of her professional life the pseudo relapse. What is the pseudo relapse? You might ask, simply put it is when the client attributes normal responses to life events as the return of their illness. This is one of the great hurdles that those of us who go through mental distress must overcome. It is so easy to let every time something goes wrong in our lives either through mistakes we make or through life trauma to fall back into illness or to blame our illness. It seems to be that it is much harder for us somehow to accept that we are humans with all the fragility that goes with being a human being. Everyone has bad days for if there were no bad days how would we know what a good day is? If we never felt sadness how would we know what happiness is? If we were never bad how would we know what good is? If we never went through inner conflict how would we know what inner peace is? By the same token if we have never been mentally broken how can we tell what mental wholeness is? In that sense having gone through mental distress and achieved recovery we can understand life in a way that a great many people never will. The reality is that one of our biggest hurdles then is ourselves, if we do not believe in our own ability to achieve recovery how can we expect anyone else to believe in us.

Like Jenny in the preceding chapter we must do the bulk of the work yes supports can be identified and put in place, yes we can go to therapists or take medication. Yes we can attend self-help groups and be part of campaigns against abuses in psychiatry but unless we are prepared to do the hard personal work to achieve our personal recovery then recovery will remain a word instead of a fact. Whilst it is true that this cannot happen in isolation from the rest of society in the present climate we often will have to make it happen despite our society. We must tackle politically areas of policy that seek to maintain us in the illness role. One of the main areas that needs to be dealt with is the benefit system. It is my contention that one of the main causes of relapse today in the UK is the arrival on the door mat of a letter from the department of social security inviting the person for a review of their disabled living allowance (DLA). DLA is the great double edged sword of the British system on one hand it has enabled many service users to achieve economic freedom, allowing them to have a far greater quality of life. On the other hand it takes this benefit away from them as soon as they show signs of recovery, this is often followed by a relapse that costs the Government even more than maintaining the persons level of income would have. Surely it makes sense to scrap this nonsense and allow people the level of income that keeps them out of the system and on the recovery road.

It is time also for professionals to get their act together they should not be agents of the State they should be the enablers of their local communities. It is their task more than any others to tackle the issue of stigma in our society. Stigma is the great disease that is destroying any chance of recovery for the many, forcing those who have mental health problems to hide their problems that only perpetuates the myths that surround mental health. Mental wellness can only be achieved in a mentally well society and the professional must be at the forefront of creating this wellness.

Politicians have a duty to all their constituents and that also means' to those who have mental health problems. It is time for them to stop taking the short-term view of mental health, responding only to the tabloid press and the ranting of individuals such as Ms Wallace. If they (the Government) cannot come on board a recovery train as the train drivers then they will surely be responsible for future generations of misery suffered by those who will have mental health problems. In the UK the Government will pass a law by the year 2000 that will allow those deemed to have a personality disorder to be held indefinitely before they commit any offence. In the UK it is common for service users who do not comply with the treatment wishes of the psychiatrist to have their diagnoses changed to personality disorder. In the UK not only will computers be year 2000 compliant so will users of mental health services. If politicians could see the sense of recovery based services then perhaps just perhaps they could help create a system of mental health services that people could go to with confidence rather than fear.

Recovery is happening and it is here to stay, it is time for all of us to embrace not just the theory or the concept but the practice and the reality of recovery. Enjoy yours.

Further Reading

Anthony, W.A. (1993)
Recovery from Serious Mental Illness: The Guiding Vision of the Mental
Health Service System in the 1990's: Psychosocial Rehabilitation Journal
Vol 16 (4))

Allott, P (2002)
Discovering Hope For Recovery From a British Perspective (submitted
for publication)

Allott, P and Carling P (2001)
Partnerships in Mental Health Directional Paper III – Principles of
Recovery for a modern Community Mental Health System, Centre for
Mental Health Policy, University of England, Birmingham

Carling, PJ (1995)
Return to Community: Building Support Systems for People with
Psychiatric Disabilities. Guilford Press, New York

Chamberlain, J (1999)
The Confessions of a Non Compliant Patient, National empowerment
Centre Newsletter

Coleman R & Smith M (1998)
Working with Voices P&P Press

Coleman R (2000)
Politics of the Madhouse P&P Press

Coleman R Baker P Taylor K
Working to Recovery P&P Press(2003)

Copeland, M (1997)
Wellness Recovery Action Planning (WRAP): Peach Press USA

Davidson, L and Strauss, J (1992)
Sense of Self in Recovery from Severe Mental Illness. British Journal of
Medical Psychology, Vol 65

Deegan, P.E. (1988)
Recovery: The lived experience of rehabilitation. Psychosocial
Rehabilitation Journal, 11, 11-19.

Deegan PE (1992)
Recovery, Rehabilitation and the Conspiracy of Hope, National
Empowerment Center, USA

Deegan, PE (1996)
Recovery as a Journey of the Heart: Psychosocial Rehabilitation Journal,
19(3)

Deegan, PE (1990)
Spirit Breaking: When Helping professionals Hurt. The Humanistic
Psychologist Vol 18 (3)

Deegan PE et al (2001)
Intentional Care: Employee Performance Standards for Client Choice
Advocates Inc, Framingham, Massachusetts

Faulkner, A (2000)
Strategies for Living: A report of user –led research into people's
strategies for living with mental distress. The Mental Health Foundation,
London

Fisher, D.B. and Ahern, L. (1999)
People can recover from mental illness. National Empowerment Center
Newsletter.
F. Scott Fitzgerald (1936)
'The Crack-up' in Esquire (New York, Feb 1936; repr in The Crack-Up,
ed by
Edmund Wilson 1945

Glover, H.M. (1999)
Challenging Mental Impotence, A perspective from Queensland,
Australia: edited Allot, P: Centre for Community Mental Health,
University of Central England. Birmingham

Harding, C.M. et al (1987)
The Vermont Longitudinal Study of Persons with Severe Mental Illness,
In : Methodological study sample and overall status 32 years later.
American Journal of Psychiatry Vol 144 (6) 718-726

Harding, C.M. et al (1992)
Chronicity in Schizophrenia: Revisited. British Journal of Psychiatry,
161:27 -37

Keil, R (2001)
Mental Health Recovery Newsletter February 2001

Leader, A (1995)
Direct Power: a resource pack for people who want to develop their own
care plans and support networks, Pavilion Publishing.UK

Leete, E (1989)
How I perceive and manage my illness: Schizophrenia Bulletin, 8, 605-
609

Meagher, J (1995)
Partnership or Pretence   A handbook of Empowerment and Self
Advocacy for consumers/Users and Survivors of Psychiatric Services,
Psychiatric Rehabilitation Association, Strawberry Hills, Australia

MIND (2001)
Fact Sheets:

Mead, S and Copeland, M (2000) What Recovery Means to Us: Plenum
Publishers, New York, NY.

Department of Health (2001)
Mental Health Policy Implementation Guide, England

O'Brien J and O'Brien L (eds) (2000)
A little book about Person Centred Planning: Inclusion Press, Ontario,
Canada.

O'Hagan M (2001)
Recovery Competencies for New Zealand Mental Health Workers. New
Zealand Mental Health Commission

O'Hagan, M (1994)
Stopovers on my way home from Mars: a journey into the psychiatric
survivor movement in the USA, Britain and Netherlands. Survivor
speaks Out, London

O'Leary & Ickovics, (1998) In Ickovics and Park (eds) Thriving: Broadening the Paradigm Beyond Illness to Health, Journal of Social Issues Vol 54(2)

OHIO Department of Mental Health

Ralph, RO; Kidder, K. and Phillips, D. Can we Measure Recovery? - A Compendium of Recovery and Recovery-Related Instruments: the Evaluation
Centre @HSRI

Ralph, RO (2000) Recovery. Psychiatric Rehabilitation Skills Vol 4(3)

Rapp, C (1998)
The Strengths Model: Case Management with People suffering from Severe and Persistent Mental Illness. Oxford University Press, New York

Reeves A (1999)
Recovery An Holistic Approach P&P Press

Smith M (2000)
Working with Self-Harm P&P Press

Smith M Coleman R Good J (2002)
Psychiatric First Aid in Psychosis P&P Press

Sullivan, P (1994)
A long and Winding Road: The Process of Recovery from severe Mental Illness. Innovations and Research.Vol 3 (3)

Tooth, B; Kalyansundarum, V; Glover, H (1997)
Recovery from Schizophrenia: A consumer Perspective: Final report to Health and Human Services Research Developments Grants Program, December 1997 (Unpublished)

Topor, A (2001)
Managing the Contradictions- Recovery from Severe Mental Disorders: Stockholm Studies of Social Work 18 Department of Social Work, Stockholm University